180 DAYS

of

SELF-CARE

FOR BUSY EDUCATORS

TINA H.
BOOGREN

Solution Tree | Press

a division of
Solution Tree

555 North Morton Street
Bloomington, IN 47404
800.733.6786 (toll free) / 812.336.7700
FAX: 812.336.7790

email: info@SolutionTree.com
SolutionTree.com

Visit **go.SolutionTree.com/teacherefficacy** to download the free reproducibles in this book.

Printed in the United States of America

Library of Congress Cataloging-in-Publication Data
Names: Boogren, Tina, author.
Title: 180 days of self-care for busy educators / Tina H. Boogren.
Other titles: One hundred eighty days of self-care for busy educators
Description: Bloomington, IN : Solution Tree Press, [2019] | Includes
    bibliographical references and index.
Identifiers: LCCN 2019017614 | ISBN 9781949539271 (perfect bound)
Subjects: LCSH: Teachers--Psychology. | Self-care, Health. | Educators. |
    Self-help techniques.
Classification: LCC LB2840 .B655 2019 | DDC 371.1001/9--dc23
LC record available at https://lccn.loc.gov/2019017614

Solution Tree

Jeffrey C. Jones, CEO
Edmund M. Ackerman, President

Solution Tree Press

President and Publisher: Douglas M. Rife
Associate Publisher: Sarah Payne-Mills
Art Director: Rian Anderson
Managing Production Editor: Kendra Slayton
Senior Production Editor: Tonya Maddox Cupp
Content Development Specialist: Amy Rubenstein
Copy Editor: Kate St. Ives
Proofreader: Sarah Ludwig
Cover and Text Designer: Abigail Bowen
Editorial Assistant: Sarah Ludwig

Acknowledgments

This book is dedicated to all the members of the Self-Care for Educators Facebook group (aka *my happy place*) as well as to the various self-care clubs meeting in classrooms, living rooms, coffee shops, and restaurants all over the world (which is a dream come true for me). I am so grateful for each and every one of you, and I am cheering you on so hard.

Solution Tree Press would like to thank the following reviewers:

Stacie Beaman
First-Grade Teacher
L. J. Daly Elementary School
Fayette, Missouri

Carmen Chavez
Fourth-Grade Teacher
Sundance Elementary School
Los Lunas, New Mexico

Maria Krum
Special Education and
   Mathematics Teacher
Valencia Middle School
Los Lunas, New Mexico

Jill Maraldo
Associate Principal
Buffalo Grove High School
Buffalo Grove, Illinois

Donna Shillinglaw
Facilitator of Professional Learning
Tyler Independent School District
Tyler, Texas

Visit **go.SolutionTree.com/teacherefficacy** to download the free reproducibles in this book.

TABLE OF CONTENTS

CHAPTER 4
Finishing Strong **105**

EPILOGUE
Create Your Own Self-Care List. . . . **135**

References and Resources **139**

Index **153**

About the Author

 **T**ina H. Boogren, PhD, is a former classroom teacher, English department chair, teacher mentor, instructional coach, professional developer, athletic coach, and building-level leader. She has presented at the school, district, state, and national levels and was a featured speaker at the International Literacy Association annual conference and Barnes & Noble's educators' nights.

Tina was a 2007 finalist for Colorado Teacher of the Year and received the Douglas County School District Outstanding Teacher Award eight years in a row, from 2002 to 2009. In addition to writing articles for the National Writing Project's *The Voice* and *The Quarterly*, she authored *In the First Few Years: Reflections of a Beginning Teacher, Supporting Beginning Teachers, The Beginning Teacher's Field Guide: Embarking on Your First Years,* and *Take Time for You: Self-Care Action Plans for Educators,* an Independent Publisher Book Awards (IPPY) gold winner in the workbooks and resources category. She coauthored *Motivating and Inspiring Students* and contributed to *Middle School Teaching: A Guide to Methods and Resources* and *Becoming a Reflective Teacher.*

Tina holds a bachelor's degree from the University of Iowa, a master's degree with an administrative endorsement from the University of Colorado Denver, and a doctorate from the University of Denver in educational administration and policy studies.

To learn more about Tina's work, visit www.facebook.com/selfcareforeducators or follow @THBoogren on Twitter and Instagram.

To book Tina H. Boogren for professional development, contact pd@SolutionTree .com.

Introduction

I don't know about you, but here's how things typically work for me: I read a compelling article or new research that gets me fired up to begin a new plan—an exercise regimen, a diet plan, an organization method, or a new appliance (hello, Instant Pot)—and I am fired up for a few weeks and then, against all hope and desire, the new plan slowly drifts away and I revert to my original habits, lamenting another failed attempt at changing my life.

That is, that used to be typical for me. It has been over three years since I turned my life around through an intentional, deliberate focus on self-care, happiness, and well-being. *Three entire years*. On that realization, I've spent considerable time contemplating why this time is different, why I'm *not* back where I started, and how I was able to truly change my life in such meaningful ways.

Here's what I know for sure: self-care and the pursuit of personal well-being and happiness is an *intentional* practice. A daily, deliberate, mindful practice. This pursuit is a constant and continual work in progress. It's not something that someone simply checks off a list and forevermore changes things. It's not a place you get to just so you can slack off and reap the benefits for an extended period of time. It's so much more difficult (but rewarding) than that. It's also not commercial or consumer based. Well-being is not found in an app or a pill or a vacation or a wine glass (although those distractions can certainly feel good for a little while). We have to *do the work*. Every single day. That work is all about three things.

1. Developing a deep, keen understanding of our own needs

2. Checking in with ourselves throughout each day

3. Responding to our individual needs with targeted action

This targeted action is individual. Just because something works for your brother or your friend or the teacher next door doesn't guarantee it will work for you. It's personal—very, very personal.

In my 2018 book, *Take Time for You: Self-Care Action Plans for Educators*, I outlined a framework that educators can use to begin their own self-care journeys. It is the same process that I used to start my own path toward wellness. And now, after that initial work, I'm committed to staying on track. One way I stay on track is by recommitting to the work every single day. I do this by journaling every morning and setting goals for that day as well as outlining my vision for the future. I've also continued keeping up with the latest research and experimenting with different strategies that I learn about through that research. This book is a result of that continued work. If you read *Take Time for You*, my hope is that this book, *180 Days of Self-Care for Busy Educators*, will help you recommit and stay on your path.

You may recognize a few of the themes from *Take Time for You*, but the individual strategies are fresh. You can incorporate them into your already established plan, thinking of them as self-care hacks—bite-sized actions that may have a huge impact on your overall well-being and happiness. If you haven't read my previous book, that's OK; you can jump right into this one and start your exploration now. I am so glad you're here, no matter where you are on your own personal journey.

Since I became intentional about my self-care, happiness, and well-being, I've learned so much. I've given myself permission to take care of my whole self so that I can truly live my very best life as an educator, wife, daughter, sister, aunt, and friend. I've never felt better than I do right now, as a middle-aged woman. Does this mean that I've been perfect with my self-care practices and commitments? Absolutely not. I still have days where I forget to drink enough water or get enough sleep, and sometimes I miss the moment because my face is buried in my phone. But I've been *on* more than I've been *off*. Where I once struggled to stay motivated and keep promises to myself, I now put myself *first*. I know that reading that statement can feel uncomfortable, but hear me out.

As educators—and parents, partners, friends, and children to adult parents—we often put everyone else's needs before our own. It can feel selfish and uncomfortable to turn the tables and put ourselves first. Trust me when I promise you it's worth it. I am a significantly better educator, wife, daughter, sister, aunt, and friend now that I've learned what I need, what I don't need, what makes me feel good, and what doesn't. I am now able to present my very best self to those I serve and those I love. You can get you there, too; that's precisely why I wrote this book.

Why Self-Care Is Crucial for Educators

I aim to share what I've learned with you, my fellow educators. Whether you are a classroom teacher, administrator, instructional coach, paraprofessional, school counselor, school social worker, special educator, or any other educator, I am your fiercest advocate. *I see you* sacrificing your own health and well-being for those you serve (whether it's your students, your staff, or your communities), and I see how it's hurting you at times.

I've been fortunate enough to work with educators in every position, in nearly every state in the United States and many provinces in Canada. I interact on social media with educators in countries like Australia and South Africa. I've learned so much about myself through those interactions, but I've also learned about you. I know that we are more alike than we are different from one another. I know the incredible number of hours you spend preparing lessons, creating professional development sessions, grading papers, communicating with parents, attending events, coaching and sponsoring, evaluating, meeting, PLC-ing with your professional learning community, and heading committees, clubs, and events. I admire you for that—but I also worry. I worry because I know that if you continue putting your own needs and happiness at the bottom of your to-do list, it will be to the sacrifice of something else—your family, your health, or your students. I want better for you. *You* want better for you.

Research shows that 93 percent of teachers report "high levels of job-related stress" (Riley-Missouri, 2018). Think about that. This means that only 7 percent of teachers do *not* feel stressed out. Seven percent! That's horrifying. Additionally, so many students enter school with significant needs stemming from trauma; educators face the very real risk of experiencing *secondary traumatic stress* (also known as *compassion fatigue*). Secondary traumatic stress looks like isolation, depression, difficulty focusing, aggression, anxiety, insomnia, excessive drinking, and changes in appetite (Gunn, 2018). Not only is this a concern for our educators, but it's a serious problem for our students as well. Students with stressed-out teachers have more behavior issues, and those students have lower overall achievement (Riley-Missouri, 2018). Our goal as educators is to make a difference in the lives of our students—both academically and social-emotionally. We cannot do that if we aren't taking care of ourselves.

Additionally, when teachers are stressed or not fully engaged when they're at work, students feel it (Granata, 2014). Teachers are the biggest influence on student engagement; research proves that (Gallup, 2014; Martin, 2006). When at least one teacher makes students feel excited about their futures, or when students feel their school is committed to their strengths, they are thirty times more likely to be engaged in their work at school (Gallup, 2014). To positively impact students, educators must be excited and engaged themselves. To feel that excitement and engagement in their work, educators *must* take care of themselves. Research shows there is a "strong connection between the personal and professional wellbeing of teachers and have reasoned that there cannot be real professional development without personal development" (Day & Leitch, 2001; O'Connor, 2008, as cited in Spilt, Koomen, & Thijs, 2011, p. 461). Consider the type of teacher you'd like your own child, niece, or nephew to have? Do you want those children to have a teacher who isn't taking care of him- or herself, or do you want a teacher who is well rested, energized, and excited to be at work every day?

School administrators have high stress levels, too. Twenty percent of principals report feeling overwhelmed (Riley, 2018), and principals report more burnout than the general population. They have more trouble sleeping and are at higher risk of depression (Robinson, 2018). School and district leaders can help create a school's culture by modeling healthy behaviors themselves, heading wellness initiatives, and supporting self-care groups within the school community. As building leaders, you set the tone. Modeling the behaviors for teachers works the way teachers must model the behaviors they want to see in their students.

This book is an invitation. I invite you to explore your own habits and practices so you can see what it feels like to put yourself at the very top of your own to-do list. I want you to consider how taking care of yourself actually better equips you to take care of your own students, staff, and family. I want you to experience how it feels to be the best version of yourself and to see with your own eyes how that makes you an even better educator. I invite you to play around with some new strategies, routines, methods, and ideas in order to see just how good you can actually feel.

How This Book Is Organized

Because most schools cycle themselves around nine-week segments, I've done the same here. Therefore, there are four main chapters, and each contains nine weeks. While this book is organized according to a traditional school year, you can jump into week one at any time. If it helps, label the table of contents according to your particular school year (as school calendars vary by district, state, and province). I've included only weekdays, which allows for some grace, some wiggle room, on the weekends for you to catch up or simply rest.

Each week, I present a new theme, invitation, and options for self-care activities that are based on the latest research. Some weeks are open to choosing strategies that speak to you, and some weeks are more structured, based on the particular theme. For the weeks that are more open, select one or two options that appeal to you—circle or highlight them directly on the page—and try them for five days. You can also write down your own ideas in the book's margins if you have another idea related to that week's theme. These invitations help you put curated research into action. When you're implementing doable daily tasks, you're making self-care a habit in a way that works for you. Very few strategies work for all people, and so part of this exploration is learning more about yourself.

Along the way, I'll share some of my own experiences and offer reflection questions at the end of each week to help you think through what worked, what didn't, and why in order to nudge you toward a life that makes you excited to jump out of bed each morning. Blank Notes pages at the end of each of the four chapters and the generous margins throughout give you room to record your overarching ideas, revelations, goals, and reflections directly in the book.

What Works for You

You'll note that I've labeled each chapter according to how most educators tend to feel during those particular months: Surviving the Season of Sacrifice (the first nine weeks), Dealing With Disillusionment (the second nine weeks), Finding Balance (the third nine weeks), and Finishing Strong (the final nine weeks; Moir, 2011). When we get a new school year started, we typically find ourselves in the season of sacrifice, where we work longer hours and adjust to the challenges of a new school year. We're often sacrificing time with our families and friends and foregoing workouts and sleep in an attempt to tackle everything school related.

During the next three months, we're typically in the throes of the dreaded disillusionment phase. Here, we're in the most challenging nine weeks of the school year. We're exhausted and struggling to keep our heads above water, student behaviors feel particularly difficult, and our emotions may be getting the best of us. Often we fall ill during this time of year, and for many of us, the weather starts to turn cold and the days offer fewer light hours. Once we return from winter break, we typically move into the season of balance, feeling more in control of our school responsibilities and less like we're drowning. Here we feel like we're on solid ground and are in a bit of a groove. Finally, during the final nine weeks of school, our aim is to finish strong. Here, even though we're dealing with state testing, spring fever, and the pressures that come with the end of the school year, we can see the light at the end of the tunnel and we're determined to close out the school year in a meaningful way.

If you discovered this book during the middle of the school year, that's great, too! You might jump into the corresponding chapter that matches how you're currently feeling, work your way to the end of the book, and then go back and start at the beginning of the next school year. Do what feels right to you.

You can do this work individually or you can team up with a single colleague or a group that can lovingly hold you accountable to the work. Partnerships like this are popular because "knowing that we will check in with someone . . . keeps us on track, even when things get hard" (Levin, 2018). You know yourself best, so consider if it's better to tackle this work on your own or if having someone else to talk to and check in with is the way to go. Also, remember that you always have a choice. If joining these invitations every week feels burdensome, allow yourself more time. There is no right or wrong way to do this. If you miss a week, it's absolutely OK. Grant yourself some grace and jump back in as soon as you can.

By working through this book in whatever order feels right, you'll begin learning how different blocks of time in the school year impact you personally. You'll learn strategies, tips, and hacks that help you survive the toughest times and that help you fully enjoy the moments where you are less stressed out and feeling good. The only way you can mess up is by not trying. Because you're here, reading this sentence right now, I know you're ready to give this a chance. I'm here beside you, cheering you on, throughout your entire journey. I encourage you to do some reflecting before starting your journey.

Take a moment to consider your current level of satisfaction when it comes to your self-care. On a scale of 1 to 10, where would you place yourself in terms of how you currently feel? Why?

....

....

Are there changes you want to make? What is your reason for wanting to make these changes?

....

....

What currently brings you joy in your life?

....

....

Who can support you on your journey? What does support from this person (or these people) look like?

....

....

What is your greatest hope in doing this work?

....

....

Are you ready? Take a deep breath. Let's do this!

CHAPTER 1

Surviving the Season of Sacrifice

Beginning this book probably marks the start of a new school year for you. If that's the case, happy new year! For these first nine weeks, we're going to explore opportunities related to our most basic physiological needs and also explore invitations that help us feel energized and truly alive as these will help set us up for success for the following weeks. Starting a new school year is filled with long days and lots of stress, whether you are a classroom teacher, instructional coach, administrator, paraprofessional, or any other position. Welcoming students and staff, adjusting to a new schedule, meeting families, and setting up your learning environment take time—hours that often come at the sacrifice of your own family, personal needs, and healthy habits. This year is going to be different, however. *This* year, you're going to glide through the first nine weeks with energy *and* newly discovered pockets of time that you never knew you had!

Week One: Music (Days 1–5)

Quick! What's your favorite song? What artist or genre gets you up off your feet (or at least tapping your toes)? Music is such a powerful tool to help us quickly change our moods. Research shows it "can reduce anxiety, depression, blood pressure, and pain as well as improve sleep quality, mood, memory, increase some cognitive functions, enhance learning and concentration, and ward off the effects of brain aging" (Hampton, 2016).

I finally decided that it was totally and completely worth it to pay the subscription cost to the streaming music website Spotify (www.spotify.com/us) because I use it every single day. I create playlists for everything I need: to get me going in the morning, to calm me down, to focus when I'm working, to use during my workshops with educators, to get me pumped up while I'm working out, and to remind me of special times or events (such as my wedding song and those I associate with vacations or milestones). I love turning up the music loud in the morning and I love putting my earbuds in at the airport, creating a soothing soundtrack for the hustle and bustle going on around me. I am so incredibly grateful for the power of music.

 This week's invitation: Put the power of music to work for you.

- **Monday:** Create a go-to good-mood playlist. Use iTunes (https://apple.com/itunes), Google Play (https://play.google.com/store/music?hl=en_US), Spotify (https://spotify.com), Pandora (https://pandora.com), Amazon Music (www.amazon.com), or whatever other tool you have to create a five- or ten-song playlist that's guaranteed to put you in a good mood.

- **Tuesday, Wednesday, and Thursday:** Now crank it up. Tap Play at different times of the day on your fabulous compilation and check in mentally to see if it impacts your mood. Does listening in the morning feel different than listening in the afternoon? Do you crave different music in the evening? Pay attention to all of these details. You might consider engaging in mindful listening, which is similar to mindful eating (page 129). To do this, close your eyes and give your full attention to the song you're listening to. Imagine what a person with *synesthesia* (sensations accompanying others, such as seeing colors when listening to music) might see or feel when listening to your songs. Write your observations about your experiences in the margins here.

- **Friday:** Share your playlist with a colleague, friend, or family member (kind of like when we used to give someone a mixed tape if you're of a certain age). Or, if you're a teacher, play at least one or two songs during class with your students. Try incorporating music into your curriculum, regardless of grade or subject. You might even consider starting lunchroom karaoke! What about a student or staff (or both) dance party in the morning or to end the day? Additionally, you could invite your students to share one of their favorite (school-appropriate) songs with you or the class as a way to get to know one another at the start of the school year. Staff could do this together as a way to build school culture and community.

  If you're an administrator, play songs during passing period or before or after school through the speaker system. See how playing music at the start of class or during passing period alters the climate. If students have an assessment, perhaps you can play some music to pump them up and get them ready before they begin. Or you could play music as a way to celebrate students' accomplishments—either the whole class' or individual students'.

  Now that you've experimented with your playlists the last few days, spread the joy today!

Reflect on the Week

When and how did you incorporate music into your
schedule this week? Which options did you choose and why?

....

....

How did the power of music impact your week?

....

....

How did sharing your playlist impact your day (and those around you)?

....

....

Do you plan to continue making music part of your routine? Why and how?

....

....

Week Two: Nutrition and Hydration (Days 6–10)

I know, I know, it's not always fun to consider how the food we put in our bodies impacts how we feel, but the truth of the matter is, taking control over what we eat can have a huge impact on our mood and overall well-being (Naidoo, 2018). I've made massive shifts in my nutrition, and the biggest—totally unexpected—payoff of doing the hard work in this area has been my happiness. By eating foods that align with my health goals, I have found that my mood has stabilized (at a good place). Because I feel good physically, my energy and stamina are at all-time highs.

All that said, it's not always easy to make the choices that I want or need to make. Of course, there's a time and a place to splurge and enjoy homemade cookies or tortilla chips and guacamole (my all-time favorite treat). I just try to limit those splurges for special occasions or situations rather than indulging regularly. On a daily basis, it's important to keep blood sugar levels balanced. Balancing blood sugar helps you avoid "adrenal fatigue, weight gain, sleep disturbances, and cardiovascular disease" (Ryan, n.d.). By balancing your blood sugar, you can move away from energy spikes and terrible crashes brought on by the sugary treats that we sometimes rely on to get through the day. This week, choose an option (adapted from Healthline Editorial Team, n.d.) that feels like a challenge but is still within reach.

 **This week's invitation:** Think about nutrition and your happiness.

- **Don't skip meals:** It's so very easy to miss breakfast when you're hustling to get out the door, or to miss lunch when you're trying to get three things checked off your to-do list during a twenty-minute lunch break. If you choose this option, commit to *not* skipping any meals. Not eating meals "makes your body less able to assimilate food" and makes you more likely to overeat at the next meal (Healthline Editorial Team, n.d.). You can try prepping meals the day before or allowing a few extra minutes in the morning to eat breakfast and pack a lunch.

Try to eat without distractions, too, so you can tune in to how stopping to eat (instead of skipping a meal or eating on the run) makes you feel. You might discover that stuffing a protein bar into your mouth while you're at the copy machine isn't nearly as satisfying as eating with intention and savoring the food.

If you're working with a partner or a team, consider sharing the load here. Perhaps one person can bring lunch to share on Monday and Tuesday and you can bring lunch to share on Wednesday, Thursday, and Friday. If your school has an active parent teacher organization (PTO), consider asking them to host a bimonthly teacher appreciation lunch with an emphasis on healthy foods.

- **Keep a food journal:** A food journal doesn't have to be complicated or burdensome. Consider keeping track of everything you eat and drink and writing down how you feel before, during, and after eating or drinking each item. You can use a notebook, a notes app, or the template in figure 1.1 (pages 15–16) to journal.

  Later, you can reflect on where your nutrition is coming from and how what you eat impacts how you feel. For example, after journaling you may notice that when you had a bagel on Tuesday, you were hungry an hour later, but when you had eggs on Wednesday, you weren't hungry until lunch. Or you might discover that on Tuesday, you reached for a sweet treat at 2:30 p.m. and that this felt good in the moment, but you crashed (and felt guilty about your choice) at 4:00 p.m. With that realization, on Wednesday you may decide you want to try an apple and some almond butter at 2:30 p.m. to see if you feel less tired (and less guilty) at 4:00 p.m. Are your food choices different on the weekend versus during the week? Do those choices impact your mood at all?

- **Drink more water:** You've heard this one before. No matter how much water you currently drink, make it your mission to increase that number by at least eight ounces. Generally, adults should drink eight ounces of water eight times per day—the 8×8 rule—because

	Breakfast	Lunch	Dinner	Snacks
Monday Food and Drink				
How I Felt	Before: During: After:	Before: During: After:	Before: During: After:	Before: During: After:
Tuesday Food and Drink				
How I Felt	Before: During: After:	Before: During: After:	Before: During: After:	Before: During: After:
Wednesday Food and Drink				
How I Felt	Before: During: After:	Before: During: After:	Before: During: After:	Before: During: After:
Thursday Food and Drink				
How I Felt	Before: During: After:	Before: During: After:	Before: During: After:	Before: During: After:

continued →

Figure 1.1: Food journal.

		Breakfast		Lunch		Dinner		Snacks
Friday	**Food and Drink**							
	How I Felt	Before: During: After:		Before: During: After:		Before: During: After:		Before: During: After:
Saturday	**Food and Drink**							
	How I Felt	Before: During: After:		Before: During: After:		Before: During: After:		Before: During: After:
Sunday	**Food and Drink**							
	How I Felt	Before: During: After:		Before: During: After:		Before: During: After:		Before: During: After:

Visit go.SolutionTree.com/teacherefficacy for a free reproducible version of this figure.

water increases our energy levels and brain function and helps prevent and treat headaches (Leech, 2017), which are a nightmare when you're trying to lead a class or staff. If you have trouble getting enough water, consider the following.

o Buy yourself a new water bottle that makes you feel good! It doesn't have to be expensive; just choose something that appeals to you so you're more apt to reach for it.

o Maybe you tend to drink more when you have a straw. I do. These days, many water bottle lids have built-in straws; you can buy dishwasher-safe stainless-steel straws that you can use again and again (and that also help save the environment). According to Bethany Blakeman (2018) of *New York* magazine, SipWell are the best regular-sized stainless-steel straws available.

o To help keep track of how much water you've drunk, secure rubber bands around the top of your water bottle, and for every bottle that you finish, move one rubber band to the bottom of your bottle before refilling. For example, if you have a thirty-two-ounce water bottle, you can put two rubber bands around the top of your bottle (because you need to drink two of those to make your sixty-four ounces). If you have a sixteen-ounce water bottle, you can put four rubber bands around the top of your bottle.

o If you love water bottles (like I do) and already own several, consider designating each to a specific time of day. For example, your blue water bottle can correlate to the morning, your clear water bottle can correlate to the afternoon, and your Colorado-flag water bottle can correspond with the evening. You then know that you have to drink the total blue water bottle by 11:30 a.m., your clear water bottle by 3:00 p.m., and your Colorado-flag water bottle before bedtime, perhaps shooting to be finished by 7:00 p.m. so you don't have to get up during the night to use the bathroom.

o Consider infusing your water with fruit, vegetables (such as cucumber), or herbs—even lavender—if you don't particularly like the taste of plain water. There are special water bottles and pitchers that help make this easy, or you can simply do it yourself.

o Use an app to track how much water you're consuming. I'm partial to Plant Nanny, found at https://apple.co/2FkAnFH, myself. Visit **go.SolutionTree.com/teacherefficacy** to find a list with live links to different apps.

Reflect on the Week

When and how did you incorporate healthy eating and hydration habits into your schedule this week? Which options did you choose and why?

....

....

Did you notice any changes—subtle or major—in your mood this week?

....

....

How did having an awareness of your nutrition choices help shape your week both professionally and personally?

....

....

Do you plan to continue to make a focus on nutrition and hydration part of your routine? Why and how?

....

....

Week Three: Sleep (Days 11–15)

Consider this: "for most adults, getting seven to eight hours of sleep tonight might be the most important thing we can do to improve our future physical and mental health" (World Sleep Day, n.d.). That's from Erik St. Louis, who is co-director of the Mayo Center for Sleep Medicine. I don't know about you, but I'm an entirely different person when I've had enough sleep versus when I haven't. When I'm well rested, I can let frustrations slide off me a bit more, I am able to make food choices that match my health goals, I feel more energized even during the dreaded 3:00 p.m. slump, and I am my best self around others. Conversely, when I haven't had enough sleep (particularly for multiple nights in a row), I'm set off by nuances, find myself drawn to carbs and sugar all day long, lack the energy and luster that I thrive on, and am somewhat unpleasant to keep company with.

Approximately one in three adults in the U.S. isn't getting the necessary seven to eight hours of sleep (Luyster, Strollo, Zee, & Walsh, 2012). Insufficient sleep is not only an issue in the United States, it is a worldwide health epidemic (Chattu et al., 2018). When you don't sleep those inconvenient but necessary and glorious hours, you get sick more easily, can't think as well, forget things, gain weight, and are more prone to car and workplace accidents (Marcin, n.d.). No, thank you!

 This week's invitation: Get at least seven hours of sleep per night. Every night.

- **Monday:** Work to keep your bedroom quiet, cool, and dark. Use earplugs if you need to, set your thermostat to around sixty-five degrees, try a fan or noise machine, and use your curtains (or a sheet) to block out the light as much as possible (Smith, Robinson, & Segal, 2018).

- **Tuesday:** Experiment with an evening snack. For some people, eating before bed can cause indigestion, but for others, a quality snack can promote a good night's sleep. Good choices for an evening snack include milk or yogurt (if your body tolerates dairy), a banana, half a turkey sandwich, or a small bowl of whole-grain, low-sugar cereal (Smith et al., 2018).

- **Wednesday:** Limit caffeine intake. Caffeine can cause sleep problems up to ten to twelve hours after consumption, so plan your last caffeinated beverage of the day to correlate with your anticipated bedtime (Drake, Roehrs, Shambroom, & Roth, 2013). I quit caffeine after 10:00 a.m.

- **Thursday:** Avoid bright screens one to two hours before your bedtime. The blue light that is emitted by your phone, tablet, computer, and TV is particularly disruptive to our ability to get a good night's sleep (Harvard Health Publishing, 2018a). Find ways to relax that don't involve screens—read, color, draw, or take a warm bath. Listening to an audiobook or podcast, cooking, and even singing can help, too (Hirschlag, 2017).

- **Friday:** Commit to waking up at the same time today as you will tomorrow. While the temptation to catch up on sleep during the weekend is appealing, the truth is that when we go to sleep and get up at the same time every day, we help set our bodies' internal clocks and optimize our sleep (National Institute on Aging, n.d.).

Reflect on the Week

When and how did you incorporate healthy sleeping habits into your schedule this week? Which options did you choose and why?

....

....

After considering the impact that sleep has on your daily life, including the ways it influences your energy level, mood, and nutrition, did you notice any changes— subtle or major—by using the sleep options this week? (For example, do you reach for different foods when you're tired? Does your mood feel more stable when you're well rested?)

....

....

How did focusing on your sleep habits help shape your week?

....

....

Do you plan to continue to make sufficient and high-quality sleep part of your routine? Why and how?

....

....

Week Four: Laughter (Days 16–20)

Laughter is the *best*, isn't it? Researcher and author Brené Brown (2010) says this about it: "Laughter, song, and dance create emotional and spiritual connection; they remind us of the one thing that truly matters when we are searching for comfort, celebration, inspiration, or healing: We are not alone" (p. 118). There's more and more research surfacing that supports the idea that laughter really *is* the best medicine. Some of the short-term benefits of laughter include stimulating our hearts, lungs, and muscles; releasing feel-good endorphins; relaxation; and reducing tension and stress (Mayo Clinic Staff, 2016). There are also long-term effects, including improved immune system, pain relief, increased personal satisfaction, and improved mood (Mayo Clinic Staff, 2016).

Besides all of these health benefits, just consider the last time you *really* laughed. My guess is that it felt really, really good to laugh. Laughter is like an instantaneous mood booster. I *love* to laugh! In fact, I try to find the humor in even the most stressful situations. (Wheel falls off my suitcase? Hysterical! Tripped on my morning walk? So funny! Rather than feeling frustrated and irritated, I try to choose laughter instead.)

 This week's invitation: Laugh, giggle, and guffaw.

- **Watch funny videos:** Try YouTube videos, sitcoms, and podcasts. Everyone has preferences, but if you're looking for new ideas, try simply searching online for funny podcasts or funniest YouTube videos.

- **Spend time with animals:** One of the best perks of having a pet is watching them do ridiculous things! I giggle every time my dog rolls around in the grass in the middle of a walk or when he goes to see who's at the front door when the doorbell rings on a TV show that we're watching. Savor those antics, and relish in the fact that petting animals even lowers your blood pressure and boosts your immunity (Johnson, Odendaal, & Meadows, 2002).

- **Be silly:** Skip around your classroom. Or hop on one foot! Do a somersault or a cartwheel. Roll down a hill. Do a silly dance. If you're brave, do this in public; if you're not, just close the curtains and lock the door!

- **Sing at the top of your lungs:** Belt it out! Pull out one of your playlists from week one (page 10) and sing along! I love to sing in the car (and it's a good thing others can't hear me) as singing to a song that I love always helps boost my mood. There's research that states that singing is, in fact, a natural antidepressant (TakeLessons, n.d.).

- **Start a Pinterest board:** Use your board to showcase all the funny things you find online. This activity may encourage you to always keep on the lookout for things that make you laugh. Ask your students to spend a week looking out for and collecting fun things to share with the class. At the end of the week, challenge one another to laugh. Don't just add to your board; go back and actually read what you've pinned when you need a boost.

- **Make a list:** Keep track of the funny things your students say (I still laugh when I think about the teacher who told me how many times she has to say, "Please stop licking your desk."). Write down funny quotes you read. Utilize them in your classroom or school. Challenge your students to share quotes of their own or anecdotes about the things that make them laugh. Research confirms that using humor to cope makes us more likely to be positive (Doskoch, 2016). During a staff or PLC meeting, have folks share the funniest thing they heard their students say or do that week.

- **Learn and share:** Learn a new joke and share it with a colleague. Ask your colleague to share a joke with you, or suggest opening a teacher meeting with each participant sharing a good-spirited joke. Telling a joke increases our sense of belonging, which is essential for building a positive school culture (Doskoch, 2016).

Reflect on the Week

When and how did you incorporate laughter into your schedule this week? Which options did you select and why?

....

....

Which options were your favorite and why? Which options didn't work for you and why?

....

....

How did focusing on laughter help shape your week both professionally and personally?

....

....

Do you plan to continue to make laughter part of your routine? Why and how?

....

....

Week Five: Technology (Days 21–25)

We love it, and we hate it. Technology can be a gift as well as a burden. Social media allows us to connect with others, share ideas, and escape for a few minutes. According to research, the average American spends two hours and fifty-one minutes on his or her phone each day (Text Request, 2017). The World Health Organization, which holds annual meetings about the topic, warns that technology addiction "has reached the magnitude of a significant public health concern" (Ladika, 2018). In fact, most of us struggle to go longer than ten minutes without checking our phones. Yikes! Looking at your phone reduces the ability to concentrate, solve problems, express creativity, pay attention, sleep, trust other people, and empathize (Lin, 2012). Read that sentence one more time. That's terrifying.

Consider for a moment how scrolling may be impacting your happiness. Psychologist Mihaly Csikszentmihalyi (2008) says the "best moments in our lives are not passive, receptive, relaxing times [but] usually occur if a person's body or mind is stretched to its limits in a voluntary effort to accomplish something difficult and worthwhile" (p. 3). I had to work hard to reduce the amount of time that I spent scrolling. I didn't realize how addicted I was until I participated in a 40 for 40 Challenge (40 for 40, n.d.), where for forty minutes a day for forty straight days, I committed to closing my laptop, turning off the TV, and hiding my smartphone during my free time. (This was when I wasn't otherwise working; technology is an essential part of my work, and it may be part of yours, too.) For me, the first ten minutes were OK, but at about the ten-minute mark I found myself automatically reaching for my phone, just as the research predicted (Lin, 2012). Once I got over that hump, though, I found myself absorbed in a novel or writing or getting active, often for longer than forty minutes—all of which I was grateful for.

 This week's invitation: Unplug for a bit.

- **Monday:** Keep a running record of how many times you pick up your phone (or whatever digital device you typically use, such as a tablet, iPad, and TV) today. Some phones track screen time for you; check under

Settings for options. Digital Wellbeing on Android devices helps track screen time, and QualityTime (www .qualitytimeapp.com) is also for Android phones; it tracks phone use per app. On Apple devices, look for the Screen Time option in Settings. Tally marks on a sticky note will do if you don't want to use technology to track your technology use.

How do you feel about the number of times you checked? To further observe your technology use, you might pay attention to how many minutes go by between each reach for your device.

- **Tuesday and Wednesday:** Purposefully choose fifteen sequential minutes in your day to unplug completely (besides when you're teaching, as I know you're fully engaged with your students during that time). Try to choose a time when you typically use a device so you can get the full experience of shutting down. Use no electronic devices whatsoever. Note when your scroll finger starts to feel twitchy.

- **Thursday and Friday:** You made it fifteen minutes the past two days. Can you make it thirty minutes (or more) today and tomorrow? Push yourself to see how long you can go and notice how it makes you feel.

Reflect on the Week

When and how did you incorporate unplugging into your schedule this week? Which options did you choose and why?

....

....

How did it feel to unplug for fifteen minutes? What did you do with this time?

....

....

How did it feel to unplug for thirty minutes? What did you do with this time?

....

....

Do you plan to continue to make unplugging part of your routine? Why and how? What about trying something like a Tech-Free Tuesday? Check out Screen-Free Week (www.screenfree.org) for more options.

....

....

Week Six: Altruism (Days 26–30)

On a work trip where everything was going horribly wrong, I approached the airline counter with tears in my eyes. The gate agent looked at me with sincerity and softly said, "I'm here to help." Those four simple words of kindness nearly melted me. I was able to catch my breath and accept help. Being kind, or giving to someone, actually decreases stress and enhances mental health (Achor, 2011a).

As I move about my days, I try to consciously engage in acts of kindness much like this gate agent did for me. Not only do *I* feel better, but I'm certain that it's having an impact on those around me as well. Lately, I've committed to engaging in at least five small acts of kindness every time I'm at the airport or the grocery store or conducting a workshop for educators. At the airport, for example, I'm always on the lookout for opportunities to help. I might help a mom with her bags as she maneuvers through the TSA line with her small children. I might allow a rushed person to go ahead of me in line. I definitely smile at everyone I make eye contact with, hold doors, and offer thanks, and all of these small moves add up to make an entirely different travel experience than the experience I have on days when I'm just going through the motions, feeling irritated by the things that are frustrating about traveling. Since setting this altruistic intention, I find myself having more good days than frustrating days, and I keep my eye on the good in the world rather than getting bogged down by the ugliness.

This week, you could choose one idea and use it every day, or mix it up—that's your call. If you're really feeling this invitation, you can certainly commit more than one act—in fact, the more, the better!

 This week's invitation: Commit one altruistic act every day.

- **Clean up for others:** Pick up litter. Rake your neighbor's yard. Help a colleague clean up his or her classroom after a special activity.

- **Communicate:** Call a student's parents and tell them something positive about their child. Check in on a colleague—particularly a beginning educator.

Communicate nonverbally; make eye contact and smile at everyone you see.

- **Share positivity:** Post a sticky note of positivity somewhere in your school. (I like to leave notes on the bathroom mirror, which works in faculty and student restrooms alike.) Mentor someone by modeling positivity. Be a respectful driver who gives everyone space and doesn't seek retribution when someone doesn't drive so respectfully or carefully.

- **Give what you can:** Give a colleague or a student a good book or article. (If you see an article about a band or topic you know a student is interested in, sharing it with him or her can help strengthen your relationship.) Give up your seat for someone else. Give a stranger or a student a sincere compliment.

- **Reward someone:** Spring for someone else's coffee. Put change in a vending machine. Leave a generous tip. Share treats with colleagues.

Reflect on the Week

When and how did you incorporate altruistic acts of kindness into your schedule this week; which options did you choose and why?

....

....

What act was your favorite act and why?

....

....

How did others react to your altruism?

....

....

Do you plan to continue to make altruism part of your routine? Why and how?

....

....

Week Seven: Wardrobe (Days 31–35)

Steve Jobs, Albert Einstein, Barack Obama, and Mark Zuckerberg all have something in common (and though they're not quite as famous, so do Matilda Kahl and Kelly Cutrone). They all chose a work uniform to eliminate *decision fatigue*, to project a certain image, and to be comfortable (Anzia, 2018; Smith, 2012). *Decision fatigue* is the notion that we all have a finite amount of mental energy when it comes to exerting self-control (Tierney, 2011).

I love this work uniform idea. I love this idea so much that I've embraced it and am experimenting with the idea of working a *capsule*, or minimalist, wardrobe, which has a handful of classic pieces of clothing that I can add to for the weather (Anzia, 2018). Since 2009, I've embraced my love of black, white, and grey clothing and have worked hard to keep a smaller number of items in my closet, subscribing to the if-I-haven't-worn-it-in-six-months-it's-gone rule. By having fewer items and only those that go with nearly every other item of clothing in my closet, I've noticed significantly less stress in my morning routine, less anxiety over the state of my closet and dresser, and less difficulty packing for work trips and vacations. I've saved myself time, space, and money—which are essentials for my self-care goals.

Prior to taking up the invitation, think about what you wear and how you make decisions about what you wear. How much time are you spending choosing your work clothes in the morning? Are you OK with this amount of time? Do you feel stressed having to get dressed? Do you try on multiple items before making your final decision, pulling or tugging them to feel comfortable?

 This week's invitation: Experiment with the idea of creating a work uniform.

- **Wear it again:** Once you have on an outfit that feels good, wear it again later this week. How does this make you feel? Does anyone notice?

- **Clean your closet:** Spend thirty minutes working on cleaning out your closet. You may need multiple thirty-minute sessions over a few days to accomplish this. Get rid of anything that doesn't fit, that isn't comfortable, or that you haven't worn in six months. You can donate those items; swap clothes with your friends, family, or colleagues; or take them to a consignment store. If you wear something to work that doesn't feel good or doesn't fit right, get rid of it immediately (donate, swap, or sell it) when you get home rather than keep it.

- **Get inspired:** Pay attention to what others are wearing to gain ideas for your own wardrobe. What colors and styles are you drawn to? Do these preferences match what you currently own? Also notice what you're wearing when you feel extra good about yourself.

Reflect on the Week

When and how did you incorporate simplifying choosing and wearing clothing into your schedule this week? What options did you choose and why?

....

....

As you went through your work day, did your clothes help you or not help you? Did you find yourself pulling or tugging them to feel comfortable, or did they serve you and your work so that you got through your day without even noticing what you were wearing?

....

....

What option worked best for you?

....

....

How do you envision simplifying your wardrobe having an impact on your life? Do you plan to continue to make wardrobe simplification part of your daily routine? Why and how?

....

....

Week Eight: Time (Days 36–40)

For a long time, I believed that I'd be happier if I just made more money or had a better car or a nicer home, and so I hustled to coach another season, run another after-school club, and sit on another committee so I could earn more money and have nice things and, therefore, be happier. What I discovered is that hustling to earn more money didn't actually make me happier. In fact, the time that I spent hustling could have been used to actually increase my happiness in a really simple way: by incorporating *time affluence* into my life.

According to researchers Ashley V. Whillans, Aaron C. Weidman, and Elizabeth W. Dunn (2016), valuing time over money is an essential key to our well-being. In fact, Whillans et al. (2016) discovered that people who prioritize time over money work fewer hours and have more time to engage in activities that they find enjoyable. In other words, we should consider slowing down and savoring the pockets of time that we have, even if that might mean that we have a bit less money and fewer things. Additionally, "passing the hours working (although productive) does not translate into greater happiness. Spending time with loved ones does, and a shift in attention toward time proves an effective means to motivate this social connection" (Mogilner, 2010, p. 1352).

Once I discovered this research, I started making subtle shifts in my decisions, opting to go for time affluence over fiscal affluence. It worked! By opting for a cleaning service to come clean our home every two weeks, my husband and I gained the gift of time together. Rather than spending our entire Saturday afternoon cleaning, we do things together that we both enjoy. Rather than overscheduling myself by saying yes to every workshop opportunity, I schedule adequate days at home in between my travel commitments. While I may earn less money in the long run, my happiness is increased.

 This week's invitation: Don't schedule yourself all available hours. Leave time for the people and things you love (including yourself).

- **Allow yourself time:** Allow yourself ten extra minutes in the morning so you don't feel rushed. Resist hitting that snooze button, and instead get up and enjoy those nine (or eighteen) minutes as part of your morning routine.

- **Schedule time:** Schedule a block of time (I recommend between thirty minutes and an hour) to do something that brings you joy. This could be anything that makes you happy: reading, going for a walk, gardening, or cooking. This time may be during your lunch break, in the morning or evening, or during the weekend if that feels more doable to you.

- **Salvage time:** If you use public transportation to commute to school, use that time to call someone, read a novel, or simply daydream instead of grading papers, revising your latest unit, or prepping for the staff meeting. If you drive to school, consider this time a luxury, and listen to your new playlist, talk radio, a podcast, or an audiobook. Or nothing. Listen to nothing at all.

- **Eat at lunch time:** Take a lunch without making parent phone calls or catching up on gradebook entries, and consider if this makes your lunch break feel longer than usual. Refer to the mindful eating option (page 129) to take this option a step further.

- **Be present at times:** As often as you can when you're with family or friends, be *fully* present rather than working at the same time. Putting your phone away is a good idea, too. I know this isn't possible during *every* interaction that we have, but being mindful of our presence with others can make our time with loved ones more memorable and special.

- **Check your time:** Look at your calendar, and consider what is essential and what is nonessential. Can you cancel or postpone something that isn't essential? Use that bonus time to do something you love. Also, commit to leaving work at a specific time each day this week. (And please don't choose 8:00 p.m. as your ending time.)

- **Use wait time:** On the other end of salvaging time, make productive use of wait time. Always have a book, crossword puzzle, podcast, or article on hand for those inevitable moments when you're stuck in line or a waiting room. I find that when I read something and resist being online instead, I feel so much better about my wait time.

Reflect on the Week

When and how did you incorporate time for things you enjoy into your schedule this week? Which options did you choose and why?

....

....

What option was your favorite and why? What option didn't work for you and why?

....

....

How did focusing on time affluence help shape your week both professionally and personally?

....

....

Do you plan to continue to make time affluence part of your routine? Why and how?

....

....

Week Nine: Mindfulness (Days 41–45)

By now, you've probably heard of, and have maybe even experimented with, mindfulness. Jon Kabat-Zinn (2003), who created the Stress Reduction Clinic and the Center for Mindfulness in Medicine, Health Care, and Society at the University of Massachusetts Medical School, defines *mindfulness* as "awareness that arises through paying attention, on purpose, in the present moment, non-judgmentally . . . It's about knowing what is on your mind" (p. 145). For me, mindfulness was something I tried for a while and then gave up on. Then I read more research about all the amazing benefits—increased self-esteem, self-control, and immunity (Büssing, Michalsen, Khalsa, Telles, & Sherman, 2012; Felver, Butzer, Olson, Smith, & Khalsa, 2015; Raes, Griffith, Van der Gucht, & Williams, 2014; Semple, Droutman, & Reid, 2017). It also decreases stress and depression (Ackerman, 2017b). So, I gave it another shot. And then I quit. Again.

It literally took years for this habit to stick with me. Today, mindfulness is a daily practice, and it takes on various forms in my life. When I'm at home, I like to take mindful walks with my dog early in the morning. I leave my headphones at home and my phone in my pocket (on hand for emergencies only) and pay attention to the feel and sound of my feet hitting the ground and my breath moving in and out. This helps me feel grounded and centered so I can tackle my day when I get back home. When I'm traveling to conduct professional development workshops, I do a five- to ten-minute meditation in my hotel room every morning. Additionally, at various times throughout the day, whether I'm at home or on the road, I pause to take three deep breaths that help to slow down a racing heartbeat, help to stabilize my blood pressure, and connect me to the present moment and what I may need to do to take care of myself right then (Harvard Health Publishing, 2018b).

As educators, our daily lives are hectic and ever-changing. It's easy to feel overwhelmed and out of control; research shows the majority of educators feel like this at times (Riley, 2018; Riley-Missouri, 2018). Mindfulness is a way to combat those feelings and feel calm, centered, and capable.

Consider the following choices, and choose one that you'd like to try a few times, or every day, this week. If you already engage in one of this week's mindfulness options, challenge yourself to try something new, either as an addition to your regular practice or perhaps in place of it for at least this one week. Another idea is to try a different option each day so you can get a feel for what works best for you and what doesn't work as well.

This week's invitation: Try at least one (new) mindfulness technique.

- **Mindful walking:** Mindfulness trainer and Mindful Schools senior program developer Oren Jay Sofer (2016) offers these eight steps to engage in a mindful walk.

    a. Choose as quiet and undisturbed a place as possible to practice. Choose a flat path that allows you to take at least ten steps. Don't worry if you live in the city; just make do with what you have.

    b. Stand at one end of your path and pay attention to your body. Try to relax and just stand; feel how natural and easy this is if you allow it to be.

    c. Now walk. Your steps should be comfortable and maybe even a little slower than usual. Your pace should let you feel your feet and legs moving.

    d. Focus on how the feelings and the sensations in your feet change as you walk. There is heaviness, pressure, movement, and even temperature— notice all of those things. Feel the contact with the ground each time you take a step.

    e. Try not to look around too much. That helps keep you focused on your insides. When your thoughts start to wander, notice that that's happening, and just return your mind to the sensations you feel as you're walking. Do this over and over again, every time your mind tries to take you somewhere else.

    f. When you're at the end of your walking path, stop and stand still. Don't turn around yet.

Feel your body as it rests. Notice how this feels different than walking.

g. When you're ready to turn around, pay attention to how that feels as well. After turning, stand still for a moment before walking in the other direction.

h. Try this for ten or fifteen minutes.

- **Guided meditation:** I find it easier to use guided meditation than to sit in silence. There are so many amazing apps. Headspace (https://headspace.com/headspace-meditation-app) is a popular one, and you can visit **go.SolutionTree.com/teacherefficacy** for links to many others. You can also check out the collection of guided meditations from the UCLA Mindful Awareness Research Center (http://marc.ucla.edu/mindful-meditations).

Consider what time of day you'd like to try this. For some people (like me), the morning feels like an essential time to get grounded for the upcoming day. For others, taking a break during the day (perhaps during lunch or during plan time) might help to re-center them. For others, meditating in the evening can be a way to relax and close out their workday before getting ready for bed.

You might also lead a four-minute guided meditation with your students like this adapted one (Mason, Rivers Murphy, & Jackson, 2019).

a. Rest the backs of your hands on your knees.

b. Close your eyes and focus on the area between your eyebrows.

c. Breathe deeply. Inhale deeply and exhale.

d. When you have a thought, think about the thought for just a moment. Then relax and let it go.

e. Do this breathing and relaxing until the teacher tells you to open your eyes.

- **Deep breathing:** Set an alarm or a reminder to stop and take a few mindful breaths at least three different times during one day. You might consider pausing once in the morning, once in the afternoon, and once in the evening. This also is something you can do with your students. You can even invite staff members to take a deep breath before starting a PLC or faculty meeting so everyone can begin feeling present in the room.

  To engage in deep breathing, try following the four steps as outlined by Anxiety Canada (n.d.).

    a. Take a slow breath in through the nose, breathing into your lower belly (for about four seconds). You'll feel your stomach expand while you're engaging in this step. (I like to place my hand on my belly so that I can feel my stomach expanding and relaxing.)

    b. Hold your breath for one or two seconds.

    c. Exhale slowly through the mouth (for about four seconds).

    d. Wait a few seconds before taking another breath. Repeat this a few times.

  How do you feel? The hope is that you feel more calm, centered, and in the present moment now. Amazing, right?

- **Silence:** A typical day at school rarely includes silence, and so this option asks you to intentionally seek it out. According to Jeanie M. Iberlin (2017), silence is a powerful stress reducer as it helps us feel calm and tranquil. Consider your daily activities and whether silence is, or can be, a part of any of them. Consider showering, brushing your teeth, making breakfast, driving to and from school, and walking in complete silence. Resist the urge to listen to the news, music, or a podcast.

- **Yoga:** For some of you, yoga is a regular practice. For others, yoga can feel intimidating, especially if you aren't flexible or bendy. (Good news—yoga isn't about being able to put your legs behind your head.) Try a few yoga poses this week. You can practice in the morning when you get out of bed or in the evening. If you're really feeling brave, you might attend a yoga class. Many gyms and studios offer the first few classes for free to new students.

Here are three simple poses to get started. The Sunrise pose is good for everyone. The Tree pose requires a bit of balance and Downward Dog asks you to move to the floor.

- **Sunrise pose:** The five steps for this pose are as cited by Annie Buckley (n.d.).

  a. Stand up tall and straight.

  b. Take four deep belly breaths. Feel your belly, not so much your lungs, going in and out as you breathe.

  c. On the fourth breath, lift your arms straight up above your head.

  d. Stretch your arms, spine, and waist up toward the sky while pressing your legs and feet down toward the ground. At the same time, lean over to one side. Make sure your top hip stays stacked on the other hip, instead of going forward.

  e. Hold this stretch for five seconds. Repeat on the other side.

- **Tree pose:** The four steps for this pose are as cited in Iberlin (2017).

  a. Stand on one foot. Imagine that your foot is attached to the floor like a tree trunk that has roots anchoring it.

  b. Bring your other foot up and rest it on your standing leg, just above your knee or where it feels comfortable (just not on your knee). Keep your eyes focused on one steady spot ahead of you.

   c. Bring both of your arms out to your sides or above your head like tree branches. You may also clasp your hands in front of your chest if this feels more comfortable.

   d. Hold this pose for five seconds. Remember to breathe. Repeat on the other leg. It's OK if you're not steady. There's a reason this is called a *practice*.

o **Downward Dog pose:** The seven steps for this pose are as cited in Iberlin (2017).

   a. Kneel on your hands and knees, with your hands just below your shoulders.

   b. Spread your fingers out wide while you press your palms into the floor.

   c. Straighten your legs and push your hips up, making an upside-down *V* shape. Your arms should be straight.

   d. Relax your neck muscles and focus your eyes between your legs, enjoying the stretch here.

   e. Slowly walk your hands back toward your feet (or step up between your hands). Because your legs are straight, you'll feel a stretch in your hamstrings.

   f. Hold this stretch for five seconds while taking deep breaths. (Your top half will be hanging over your legs.)

   g. Gently unroll your spine, and slowly stand as you exhale.

Ta-da—you've accomplished your first nine weeks! You might take a moment to look back over all the challenges and consider which ones have stuck, which you'd like to revisit later on, and if you're noticing any changes in your overall happiness and well-being yet. You can record your thoughts on the Notes page on page 45.

Reflect on the Week

When and how did you incorporate mindfulness into your schedule this week? Which options did you choose and why?

....

....

How did practicing the option or options impact your week?

....

....

How did focusing on mindfulness help shape your week both professionally and personally?

....

....

Do you plan to continue to make mindfulness part of your routine? Why and how?

....

....

·NOTES·

CHAPTER 2

Dealing With Disillusionment

Typically, the second quarter is a challenging time of the school year. The excitement that accompanies the start of the school year begins to slide into the overwhelm of parent conferences, never-ending to-do lists (both at school and at home as the holidays approach), finals, and exhausting commitments after the school day. Ellen Moir (2011) calls the phases associated with this time of year *survival* and *disillusionment*. And while Moir (2011) says this in the context of how new teachers feel, many educators (myself included) make the point that these phases aren't unique to beginning teachers.

You may be struggling to find balance, to find time for yourself, and to stay positive. To combat these challenges, we're going to focus on simple ways to keep our heads up and our attitudes hopeful for the next nine weeks. When things get tough, you may be tempted to set this book aside. I beg you—*don't do that*! Instead, fight for this, and commit to doing one small thing for yourself each and every week (or better yet, every single day) as a way to make it through this challenging time of year intact. Don't give up now. Dig in, recommit, and promise yourself that you're going to continue with this work!

Week Ten: Time Use (Days 46–50)

I discovered Angela Watson, a fellow educator and teacher advocate, and have relied on her time-saving tips for educators. I hope you find some relief in these as well. Since discovering her tips, I've eliminated unintentional breaks when I'm working on a presentation or writing, and I've rearranged my to-do lists to tackle my biggest tasks when I'm fresh, in the morning, rather than putting them off until later in the day, when I'm tired. I'm also continually working on overcoming my perfectionist tendencies. Rather than going over a presentation a million times (sadly, that's only a *slight* exaggeration), I check in after one or two run-throughs and then trust that I'm prepared. Some of the following are adapted from Angela Watson (as cited in Gonzalez, 2015), and there are options from other sources here as well.

 This week's invitation: Try a new or different way of managing your time.

- **Eliminate unintentional breaks:** During your plan time, set a timer and commit to actually getting done what you need to get done. It can be so easy to become distracted by social media, email, and colleagues. Work without distractions for a designated period of time, and when the timer goes off, take a break.

- **Figure out the main thing and tackle it first:** What is the number-one thing that you need to get done today? Start there. Sometimes we avoid doing The Thing because it feels daunting. Instead, we putter around with other, smaller things. Instead, prioritize the main thing that you need to accomplish and just do it. It will feel so good to be done with it!

- **Work ahead by batching:** Can you do all of your photocopying for the week on one day rather than making multiple trips throughout the week? Can you set aside a chunk of time to answer your emails all at once rather than tackling them little by little all day long? Can you plan an entire unit rather than just thinking about individual lessons?

- **Resist perfectionism:** Don't let perfect be the enemy of good. Can you relax your standards just a smidge so that you earn a little bit of time back for yourself? Rather than adjusting your lesson over and over and over again, can you trust that the key points are there and that's enough?

- **Schedule your time carefully:** Rather than working for most of your waking hours, use your calendar to carefully schedule your time and stick to it. Perhaps you give yourself two hours for planning on Sundays. Allow yourself those two hours and then be done.

- **Change your feedback:** Save time by giving personalized verbal feedback to students rather than writing all of your feedback (Hillman & Stalets, 2019). Carefully consider what work needs your careful attention and what just needs a glance. You can gain invaluable time by reconsidering your feedback options.

- **Enlist students and volunteers:** Take advantage of students who want to help or parent volunteers who visit your school. Perhaps they can make copies, decorate a bulletin board or display case, hang up student work, or sharpen pencils.

- **Use a traffic app:** I'm amazed at how much time I save when I use Google Maps (https://apple.co/2Zzsq74) or the Waze app (www.waze.com) to get me to my destination—even if I know exactly where I'm going. Because those apps can detect traffic jams and hold-ups in real time and suggest shortcuts for you, you can gain significant time that would otherwise be spent feeling frustrated in your car!

Reflect on the Week

When and how did you incorporate time management into your schedule this
week; which options did you choose and why?

....

....

How did practicing your options impact your week?

....

....

How did focusing on time management help shape your week both professionally
and personally?

....

....

Do you plan to continue to make time management part of your routine? Why
and how?

....

....

Week Eleven: Relationships (Days 51–55)

Relationships are an essential part of our overall health and well-being. As humans, we are wired for connection (Cacioppo & Patrick, 2008; Ryan & Deci, 2000a, 2000b). In fact, having healthy relationships with others can lessen our stress, help us heal from a procedure or illness, get us to engage in healthier behaviors, contribute to a greater sense of purpose, and even make us live longer (Northwestern Medicine, n.d.). According to Matthew D. Lieberman (2013), our brains have three neural networks that push us toward social connection: (1) one has to do with feeling both social pain and pleasure, (2) one helps us read other people's emotions and predict their behavior, and (3) one helps us grasp cultural beliefs and values. Additional research finds that extreme loneliness actually increases a person's chances of dying prematurely (Bergland, 2014). Those same researchers find that when someone feels lonely and isolated, he or she may have trouble sleeping, experience elevated blood pressure, have higher cortisol rates, suffer from depression, and feel a lower sense of overall well-being.

It can be easy to become isolated when we're working hard and to isolate ourselves when we're feeling stressed out or overwhelmed, but we should do the opposite. Lean on your support systems and loved ones in times of stress, and return the favor to those you love. As an introvert, I need a lot of time alone to recharge and find my balance, but I also know how much I value my relationships. I schedule time with those I love and am careful to stick to my commitments. I'm talking about face-to-face or voice-to-voice connection, here. Be intentional about balancing online connections with in-person connections. Staying connected online is nice, but it's essential that we also connect with others in 3-D.

And finally, let's talk about your students. Much has been said about how a positive relationship between teachers and students can boost student well-being and academic achievement (O'Connor, Dearing, & Collins, 2011). It stands to reason that those positive relationships also boost a teacher's well-being. It works the same way with principals and teachers (Daly &

Finnigan, 2010). The research shows that "conflictual or alienated relationships exert a threat not only to teachers' professional success but also to their *personal* wellbeing" (Spilt et al., 2011, p. 461).

 This week's invitation: Focus on your relationships, both inside and outside of school.

- **One-on-one time:** Schedule a coffee date with someone you haven't seen in a while. Plan a surprise date night with your significant other. Plan to do something before or after school with a colleague. Schedule a one-to-one conference with a few students per week. In addition to providing learning feedback, you can ask students what they like to do in their free time—this works for teachers, counselors, paraprofessionals, and administrators alike.

- **Emotional intelligence:** Take workshops (or, as an administrator, secure staff professional development) about emotional intelligence; searching online will turn up many results. This skill can improve our relationships and psyches (Vesely, Saklofske, & Leschied, 2013).

- **Long-distance communication:** Plan a Zoom (https://zoom.us) or Skype (www.skype.com/en) session with a friend or family member who lives far away. I love that technology allows us to see one another even when we can't be together in the same room.

- **Clubs:** Start a book club, Bunco group, walking club, or card, trivia, or Karaoke night with friends outside of school as well as colleagues from work so your social groups can get to know one another. Host a potluck dinner party with your neighbors, or have your friends over and make dinner together using only the ingredients you already have on hand.

- **Game nights:** Invite friends over for game night. There are lots of options beyond Monopoly and charades. Codenames and Catan are competitive board games, and Hanabi and Sentinels of the Multiverse are cooperative games (where everyone works together toward a common goal). Or maybe you start up a game of UNO with your colleagues during lunch.

- **Others:** Play at the park with your family. Play softball, kickball, or tag with your students at recess, or start a game of Wiffle Ball or pickleball after school with family or friends.

- **Volunteerism:** Join a friend, family member, or colleague you want to get to know outside school, and help your neighborhood or greater community. Try VolunteerMatch (www.volunteermatch.org) to find a good fit.

Reflect on the Week

When and how did you incorporate focusing on relationships into your schedule this week? Which options did you choose and why?

....

....

How did your chosen options impact your mood this week?

....

....

How did focusing on your relationships both inside and outside of work help shape your week both professionally and personally?

....

....

Do you plan to continue to make focusing on your relationships part of your routine? Why and how?

....

....

Week Twelve: Gratitude (Days 56–60)

By now, you've probably heard about the benefits of gratitude, which include improved physical and psychological health, enhanced empathy, and reduced aggression, as well as improved sleep and esteem (Emmons & McCullough, 2003). A study in the *Journal of Personality and Social Psychology* reports that people who write about their gratitude rather than their negative or neutral life events show greater signs of emotional well-being (Emmons & McCullough, 2003).

For me, gratitude is a daily practice. Yes, *daily.* Gratitude makes me appreciate the good days and pulls me out of negativity on the days that I'm struggling. When I'm particularly stressed or feeling blue, gratitude reminds me to take a step back and refocus my attention on the positive rather than ruminating on the negative.

 This week's invitation: Practice gratitude every single day.

- **Monday:** First thing in the morning, record three things that you're grateful for. You can record these in a journal, in your planner, or even in a note on your phone or computer. Try to think beyond the obvious (friends, family, clean drinking water) if possible, and consider recording gratitude for less obvious things like hazelnut-flavored coffee, the smell of your shampoo, or that ratty old sweatshirt you've had since college.

- **Tuesday:** Take a photo of something you're grateful for. You can share the photo on social media with the hashtag *#gratitude*, or you can simply save the photo so you have it to reflect on later. (This is a practice that I employ every single day of the year. I have photos of random things like the Denver skyline taken on my morning walk and a funny sign I saw in a parking lot in Florida reminding me to not feed the alligators.)

- **Wednesday:** Send a text expressing your gratitude for someone. You might thank a colleague for something they've done to support you, or you can reach out to a friend to say that you're especially grateful for something he or she has done for you. The more specific you are in your message, the better as it's those details that usually mean the most to us.

- **Thursday:** Right before you go to bed, record three things you're grateful for. Again, you can record these in a journal, planner, phone, or computer (though the last two might not be ideal right before bed). Consider whether it feels any different to do this in the evening versus right when you wake up, as you did on Monday.

- **Friday:** Write a handwritten note of thanks to someone. You can either deliver the note (and perhaps read it aloud to the recipient) or stick it in the mail. Consider whether this feels different than sending a text, as you did on Wednesday.

Reflect on the Week

When and how did you incorporate gratitude into your schedule this week? Did you complete all five options this week, and if not, what got in your way?

....

....

How did having an attitude of gratitude impact your week?

....

....

How did focusing on recording your gratitude help shape your week both professionally and personally?

....

....

Do you plan to continue to make gratitude part of your routine? Why, how, and when?

....

....

Week Thirteen: Saying *No* (Days 61–65)

As a perpetual people pleaser, learning how to say *no* has been an ongoing practice for me. I find myself compelled to say *yes* before I even consider the impact of my answer. Then I end up feeling resentful at the person who asked for my help, frustrated by this new thing taking up my time and completely overwhelmed because I'm trying to juggle far too many things at once and wishing I had more time for myself.

This inability to say *no* may be connected to confidence since "people with low confidence and self-esteem often feel nervous about antagonizing others and tend to rate others' needs more highly than their own" (Collingwood, 2018). As I've worked on my own self-esteem (see *Take Time for You*), I find it easier and easier to say *no*. I think that saying it is a way that we can set loving but firm boundaries for ourselves. As I've learned to honor myself and appreciate who I am, I have a clearer vision of what I want to be part of and what I want to let go of. If it's not a *heck yes*, it needs to be a *heck no*. Otherwise, when we continually say *yes* rather than stopping to consider whether it's a good idea or in line with our own goals and values, we end up feeling exhausted and irritable.

The next time someone asks you to do something that you don't want to do (or *can't* do), practice these tips. Then consider how you feel immediately afterward *and* a day or two later.

 This week's invitation: Practice saying *no*.

- **Keep your response simple:** There's no need to go on and on about why you're not jumping on board. Practice saying these statements so they feel comfortable coming out of your mouth (Collingwood, 2018).

    o "Thank you for thinking of me, but that won't work for me."

    o "My heart says yes, but my calendar says no."

    o "My other commitments don't leave time for this right now."

- **Offer an alternative:** If you provide a solution, it might feel easier, and it helps the other person (Doland, 2019). For example, you could say, "Have you talked to Erica about how interested she is in the project? We talked about it a couple days ago."

- **Buy some time:** Rather than replying *yes* automatically, buy yourself some time: "Can I get back to you by Wednesday?" Now you have time to consider if this is a *heck yes*. Do get back to this person, though; don't just leave him or her hanging to avoid having to actually say *no* (Vozza, 2016).

- **Consider a compromise:** For example, if someone wants you to cover his or her supervision duty at school, you could reply with, "Yes, I can take over your bus duty this week if you can cover my hall duty next week." Win-win (Collingwood, 2018).

- **Separate refusal from rejection:** It's important to remember that you're not rejecting a *person*—you're simply turning down a request. Remember this when the tables get turned, too (Collingwood, 2018).

- **Be true to yourself:** Honor yourself. Know what your own priorities and goals are and set boundaries around your time so you can achieve your goals. Continue building your own self-esteem so that this gets easier and easier (Blikman, n.d.).

Reflect on the Week

When and how did you incorporate boundaries into your schedule this week; what did you say *no* to and why?

....

....

Which activity option helped you say *no*, and how did it help?

....

....

How did saying *no* make you feel in the moment; a day later; a few days later?

....

....

Do you plan to continue making *no* part of your routine? Why and how?

....

....

Week Fourteen: Inspiration (Days 66–70)

This may sound lofty, but it is absolutely possible to seek out inspiration in even the most mundane days—yes, even when we're stuck in line at the grocery store or the post office. Don't believe me? Welcome to week fourteen. This week you're going to commit to helping yourself feel inspired. Who doesn't want to feel inspired? I'd much rather feel that than bored or anxious. When we feel inspired, we feel full of possibility and hope. We feel like a fire has been lit under us; we feel motivated and propelled to act.

I saw the award-winning (and brilliant) author George Saunders give a lecture at the University of Denver, where he talked a lot about his writing process and the power of the written word. I left that event feeling inspired to recommit to my own writing—and I did. When I listened to Saunders speak, I found myself thinking, "I can do that, too" and "Yes, yes, that's *exactly* how I feel, too." Thus, I felt moved to do something in my own life. Scott Barry Kaufman (2011), scientific director of the Imagination Institute, explains that feeling this way: "Inspiration awakens us to new possibilities by allowing us to transcend our ordinary experiences and limitations. Inspiration propels a person from apathy to possibility, and transforms the way we perceive our own capabilities."

When you're not sure whether the everyday can inspire you, consider that George Saunders says he was inspired to write stories when he was at the mall (as cited in Eric, 2019):

> *At another visit in the mall I was walking along and there were these two kind of Syracuse working class young women walking near me and I could hear them talking to each other. . . . I went home and I just said I'm going to try to imitate those girls.*

This week's invitation: Inspire yourself.

- **Change your environment:** Go to a different coffee shop, grocery store, or library this week.

- **Learn something new:** How about learning ten words in a different language, some astronomy, or your city's history? How about learning how to juggle?

- **Create a vision board:** Think about your big dreams and desires, and find pictures that represent those visions—you can do this the old-fashioned way on paper or poster board or via an online site like Pinterest (www .pinterest.com). If you chose the option to make a humor board on Pinterest back in week four (page 23), refer to it.

- **Visit your local bookstore or library:** Cruise the shelves, looking at all the interesting titles, images, and ideas. Recall the last book you read that you loved. Why did you love it? Find another book by the same author, on the same subject, or that takes place in the same setting. Brainstorm a list of the things you would love to learn but have never pursued. Search for books (or other resources) on one of these things.

- **Try a new art form, or listen to a new type of music:** Trying a new art form can help. If you typically like to write, try painting; if you usually play music, try writing a poem. If you typically write poetry, try writing an essay or a short story, sketching in your journal, or taking some photos in nature.

  Seek out music that isn't what you usually listen to and see what you think. What about jazz, country, classical, or dance music? Explore a type of music you may have never heard of. Have you tried chap hop (hip hop and steampunk) or babymetal (Japanese pop music and heavy metal)? Did you know that classical cellist Yo-Yo Ma has a bluegrass album titled *The Goat Rodeo Sessions*?

- **Keep an inspiration notebook:** When an idea strikes, you want to write it down so you don't forget it! Keep a notebook (or make a note on your phone) for these very moments. If you prefer to try drawing, keep a sketchbook.

- **Follow ten people on social media who inspire you:** Who are your creative idols? Go find them and follow them on Twitter (or other social media sites) so their work can continue to inspire you. I follow many of my favorite authors and speakers, like Anne Lamott, Brené

Brown, Elizabeth Gilbert, Jen Hatmaker, and Oprah Winfrey. Their posts inspire me.

- **Go beyond your comfort zone:** Nudge yourself out of your usual routine. Try something you've never done before that pushes you out of your comfort zone. Maybe hit up a Zumba class or a poetry reading, or participate in a new sport.

- **Read an autobiography or memoir by someone you admire:** Hearing about another person's struggles, triumphs, and challenges can be incredibly inspirational. It doesn't have to be about someone who's famous, either. *Educated: A Memoir* (Westover, 2018), *The Glass Castle* (Walls, 2006), and *When Breath Becomes Air* (Kalanithi, 2016) are incredible memoirs written by individuals who are not known by most people.

- **Watch an inspiring TED Talk:** TED Talks were created to be inspirational. There are so many inspiring talks out there on nearly every subject imaginable—go explore. Some of my lesser-known favorites follow.

  - Shawn Achor's (2011b) "The Happy Secret to Better Work" (https:// bit.ly/1HgldgF)

  - Ingrid Fetell Lee's (2018) "Where Joy Hides and How to Find It" (https://bit.ly/2x20xva)

  - Elizabeth Gilbert's (2009) "Your Elusive Creative Genius" (https://bit.ly/1Bt6I0j)

Watching movies can really inspire us, too; choose wisely and tuck in. Maybe seek suggestions from your students or colleagues.

Reflect on the Week

When and how did you incorporate seeking inspiration into your schedule this week? Which options did you choose and why?

....

....

Did any of the options help you feel more inspired? If so, how, and what were you inspired to do?

....

....

How do you act when you feel inspired versus when you feel you're in a rut?

....

....

Do you plan to continue to make seeking inspiration part of your routine? Why and how?

....

....

Week Fifteen: Help Requests (Days 71–75)

Now that you've conquered the challenge of saying *no* (see week thirteen, page 58), I invite you to tackle the sometimes-uncomfortable experience of asking for help. Often, we avoid asking for help because we don't want to look weak, but here's the deal: asking for help isn't weak. It's a sign of *strength*—strength because we know our own limits and we know we can't do all of it all by ourselves. Listen, I get it. I'm *terrible* at asking for help. For me, the perpetual people pleaser, it feels like I'm putting someone else out or overstepping my bounds in some way, or—*gasp!*— appearing needy or like I can't really do it all. But remember, the people who care for us *want* to help. They really do.

Turn the tables for a minute and consider if helping those in your inner circle makes you see those people as weak or needy, or if you actually see them as *human* and feel honored to help when you can. See? The key is "knowing when to ask for help and understanding why you need it," and that's exactly what we're going to explore this week (Rizzo, 2017). Whether it's asking for help with responsibilities around the house or stepping back—or completely away—from a bigger project, you have options.

 This week's invitation: Ask for help.

- **Change your mindset:** Let go of the notion that you have to do it all (Rizzo, 2017). You are absolutely worthy of the gift of receiving help. Period.

- **Reassess your priorities:** Consider who and what are most essential to you and your well-being, and consider how much time you're giving to that thing or that person. Is it enough? Do you need to rearrange some things to give more attention to the things and the people that matter the most to you?

- **Be specific:** Make sure that you're clear with your helper about why you're asking for help specifically from him or her. This will help them feel more invested in your request and actually want to help (Herrera, 2018). Also be clear about what exactly you need to avoid further frustration from possible misunderstandings.

- **Request professional development that speaks directly to self-care:** Ask the school's counseling staff or social worker (or me!) to provide professional development that speaks directly to self-care and touches on topics such as compassion fatigue (Gunn, 2018). This phenomenon occurs when a person often works with someone who has experienced trauma, which is prevalent in students (Robert Wood Johnson Foundation, 2017; World Health Organization, 2016). A schoolwide or districtwide wellness program can make a difference.

- **Take advantage of your employee assistance program:** The research confirms high stress levels in educators, and self-care is one remedy (Gunn, 2018; Riley, 2018; Riley-Missouri, 2018). However, sometimes we need something more. Contact your employee assistance program (EAP) if you are feeling acute stress or are having addiction issues. The program, if your school or employee-based insurance offers it, can connect you to mental health professionals.

Reflect on the Week

When and how did you incorporate asking for help into your schedule this week; which options did you choose and why?

....

....

How did it feel to ask for help and to receive help, and what did you discover by asking?

....

....

Did asking for help lead to you spending more time on your biggest priorities?

....

....

Do you plan to continue to make asking for help part of your routine when necessary? Why and how?

....

....

Week Sixteen: Comfort (Days 76–80)

Have you heard of *hygge*? Can you even pronounce it? I struggled with this for a while but finally learned that it's said like this: *HUE-guh*. It's a Danish concept that defines not a material object, but a *feeling*. The feeling of "cozy contentment and well-being found through enjoying the simple things in life" (Matthews, 2018). Think about enjoying a book while curled up on your sofa with a cup of hot tea while the rain comes down outside. *That* kind of cozy comfort. Ah—sounds delicious, doesn't it? This concept (and the accompanying book, *The Little Book of Hygge* by Meik Wiking [2017]) took the U.S. by storm. (Do a quick online search and you'll see what I mean.)

 This week's invitation: Get cozy.

- **Monday:** When you're at home, turn off the overhead lights and opt for candles or lamps instead (you can do this at school, too, although you should be careful with candles!).

- **Tuesday:** As soon as you get home from work, change into comfortable clothes. Yes, we're talking sweats, sweatshirts, thick socks, and those worn-out but well-loved slippers.

- **Wednesday:** Indulge in some hygge food or drinks. What food item or beverage makes you think of comfort? Is it macaroni and cheese? Tomato soup and grilled cheese? Hot tea? Cocoa? Make it happen.

- **Thursday:** Engage in an activity that feels especially comforting to you (and no, I don't mean scrolling through your phone). Is it reading? Playing a board game with your family? Strumming the guitar? Doing a crossword puzzle? Having a movie night? Choose something and commit to it.

- **Friday:** Consider how you can bring comfort to school. Wear a cozy scarf to work, or bring one of your favorite mugs from home. Create a cozy reading nook lit with tree lights, or read with your students with your shoes off so you can wiggle your toes around in your favorite wooly socks (Gilman, 2018).

Reflect on the Week

When and how did you incorporate comfort into your schedule this week? Which options did you choose and why?

....

....

How did focusing on comfort make you feel? What senses seem to be most important for you?

....

....

After having tried one or more of the options this week, what does comfort mean to you, and did trying the options help you define or redefine its meaning?

....

....

Do you plan to continue to make comfort part of your routine? Why and how?

....

....

Week Seventeen: Social Media (Days 81–85)

Social media gets a bad rap—and for good reason. It can be a total time suck. The average person spends nearly two hours on social media every day, which translates to a grand total of five years and four months total in a person's life (Asano, 2017). Let me repeat that for the people in the back: the average person is giving up over *five years* of his or her life to social media! We know that social media is designed to be addictive (Addiction Resource, 2017) and can lower self-esteem levels by making us feel bad when we compare our real lives with the filtered, photoshopped, so-called perfect lives of those we follow on social media (Jan, Soomro, & Ahmad, 2017). Social media also creates or worsens issues like cyberbullying and fake identities (Strober, 2016; Walton, 2017). This is all true, and we've probably all experienced these negative consequences of social media to some degree—but I have good news. We can take control of our newsfeeds and make social media work *for us* rather than the other way around. What role does social media play in your life? How do you feel about this platform and your relationship with it?

I participated in Offline October (https://offlineoctober.com) and stayed away from my personal social media accounts for one full month. Was it difficult? In the beginning, it absolutely was. By about week two, though, it felt good. When I entered November and came back to my social media accounts, I was able to change my habits so I didn't feel addicted, and I got to enjoy the good parts of social media (like pictures of my friends' sweet children and puppies) while treading around the not-so-good parts (like political posts).

 This week's invitation: Manage your social media use.

- **Monday:** Rather than mindlessly scrolling all day long, schedule your screen time (Wolff, 2016). Decide what time of day you're going to engage and for how long, and then stick to it. Consider limiting yourself to two fifteen-minute segments or one longer segment of thirty minutes. Set a timer for yourself when you log on, and when that timer goes off, be done.

- **Tuesday:** Be super selective about who you follow (Wolff, 2016). Stay engaged while you scroll, and tune in to how you feel or react when you see certain people's or group's posts. If you feel anxious, angry, or frustrated, you have every right to delete, unfollow, or hide them from your feed. Consider Anne Lamott's (2017) sage advice: "Don't compare your insides to someone else's outsides."

- **Wednesday:** Schedule in-person time (Wolff, 2016). Rather than fulfilling our needs for connection via social media, connect with your friends and family members in other ways. Emailing, texting, calling, or face-to-face feels much more personal and special than a comment under a post.

- **Thursday:** Stop and think before you post (Wolff, 2016). It is incredibly tempting to turn to social media when we're angry, want to vent, or feel frustrated, but that usually doesn't lead to positive results. Instead, train yourself to stop before you post. Before you put it out there, ask yourself the following questions (Brosh, 2016): "Why do I want to share this? Who will see this? Would I want this on the front page of the *New York Times?* How will others feel when they see this? What do I expect from this post?"

- **Friday:** *What do you want to pay attention to?* I have that question as the lock screen on my phone. I learned this hack from Catherine Price's (2018) incredible book *How to Break Up with Your Phone: The 30-Day Plan to Take Back Your Life.* Every time I reach for my phone, this quote stares at me and forces me to consider what I truly want to focus on in that exact moment. Sometimes it is indeed my phone, but other times I realize that I'd much rather keep my eyes up so I don't miss what's going on around me.

Reflect on the Week

When and how did you incorporate thoughtful, conscientious use of social media into your schedule this week? Which options did you choose and why?

....

....

How did changing your social media habits impact your daily routine? Did you notice any changes?

....

....

How did changing your social media habits impact the quality of your in-person conversations with others? Did you notice any changes?

....

....

Do you plan to continue to make thoughtful, conscientious use of social media part of your routine? Why and how?

....

....

Week Eighteen: Habits (Days 86–90)

Habits are powerful. On the one hand, they help give us the mental space to not have to think about every move we make; on the other hand, not all habits are good for us, and we know it—but we still can't seem to make better choices because those bad habits are so deeply engrained. Consider that "more than 40 percent of the actions you perform each day aren't actual decisions, but habits" (World Counts, n.d.). Think about a typical workday and all the habits that are embedded in that twenty-four-hour period—waking up, brushing your teeth, showering, eating breakfast, driving to work, logging in to your computer—and that's just the start of your day.

As you consider your habits, make note of which habits are healthy and which aren't so healthy. For example, I have a healthy habit of drinking a full cup of water right when I wake up in the morning. I also had a not-so-healthy habit of eating foods on the weekends that didn't align with my goals. As I began understanding the structure of a habit—cue to routine to reward—I was able to work on changing the habits that weren't serving me (Duhigg, n.d.; Rubin, 2015). A *cue*, or *trigger*, is something that sets off a habit; it might be a certain time of day, place, person, or emotional state. From there, routine kicks in based on the specific cue, and that leads us to a reward of some sort that makes and solidifies the habit.

For example, my alarm going off in the morning is a cue. That alarm cues me to get up, go to the bathroom, and throw back a full glass of water. The reward is that when I drink that water, I feel more awake; that reinforces the habit. On the other end of the spectrum, one of my cues is the weekend, where I feel more relaxed and at ease. This state of mind and this time of the week set off a routine of making food choices that are different from what I typically reach for during the week, and the reward I get is that rebel feeling of indulging in delicious food that makes me feel relaxed. The habit loop here is strong (just as it is with my water habit in the morning), but it isn't helping to serve my long-term goals, and so it's a habit that I want to change. The cue isn't going away, so I have to change the *routine* so I get my reward from a different source. I rebuilt that habit loop. The steps, adapted from doctor of Chinese medicine Teri Goetz (2016), outlined this week will help you identify one habit that you want to change and take steps to do just that.

 This week's invitation: Try changing one habit.

- **Monday:** Identify a habit that isn't serving you. Keep track of your daily habits, and choose one habit that you'd like to change. Don't beat yourself up about it; just choose one thing and commit to making a change this week.

- **Tuesday:** Identify the cue or trigger and the reward. What is the cue that sets your habit into motion, and what is the reward that you're getting out of your chosen habit? Is it comfort? Stress release? Distraction? Numbness?

- **Wednesday:** Change your routine. Once you've identified the cue and the reward that you're seeking by engaging in your typical habit, choose a different routine. In other words, how can you seek comfort in a way that better serves you? Plan your new routine when your cue is set off.

- **Thursday and Friday:** Keep trying. This isn't a magical process that will be totally taken care of in one short week. Habits take weeks to change, so acknowledge the baby steps you're taking, and if you fall into your old habit, forgive yourself and recommit to trying again.

Congratulations—you made it to the halfway point! I encourage you to take some time to review the last nine weeks and consider which invitations made a difference in your life, which you'd like to try again, and what you're noticing in terms of your personal happiness and overall well-being. Again, you can record your thoughts on the Notes page on page 76. You should be proud of yourself, even if you've missed days or weeks along the way. It's OK. Remember to give yourself the gift of grace and simply jump back in again.

Reflect on the Week

When and how did you incorporate habit-changing work into your schedule this week? Which habit did you choose to change and why?

....

....

What did you learn about the cues that set your targeted habit into motion and about the reward for engaging in that habit?

....

....

What alternate routines did you identify? How did it go this week in terms of changing that routine?

....

....

Do you plan to continue to make a practice of changing habits that don't serve you; why and how? What additional habits do you want to change, and what new habits or routines will you attach to them?

....

....

· NOTES ·

CHAPTER 3

Finding Balance

Welcome to the next phase of the school year. I think you'll like it here. These nine weeks are all about finding balance. In general, most educators return from winter break and start to move out of the tough disillusionment phase into a more relaxed, enjoyable time of the school year. A bit of time off from school hopefully was an opportunity to catch your breath and reconnect with yourself and your loved ones. Ideally, you were able to get some well-deserved sleep, and the promise of a New Year's resolution might help you kick-start these next nine weeks. During this time, we're going to get you back in your groove. You should see your students starting to show some growth here, and your focus will be on striving for calm and balance between your professional life and personal life.

The invitations for the next nine weeks are all about helping find your stride again—particularly as you recover from the disillusionment phase of the previous nine weeks.

Week Nineteen: Creativity (Days 91–95)

Do you consider yourself creative? How do you personally define creativity? What role does creativity play in your daily life? While many of us might think of creativity as something that we dip our toes into from time to time, it's actually an essential component to our overall happiness. According to neurology professor Richard Restak (2009, as cited in Kashyap, 2018), "Creativity is critical to solving problems in all parts of our lives." And you might have to think creatively to come up with ideas to practice creativity. Challenging yourself not to spend more than, say, $40 a week is a new way to frame problem solving and creativity.

For a long time, I didn't think that I was very creative. Then, as I pushed myself to try new things, I discovered that I *did* have a creative side. These days my creativity shows up in my writing, art collages, and photo gallery designs in our home.

We *all* have a creative side. Experiment with one or two of the following strategies (adapted from Heston, 2019).

 This week's invitation: Tap into your creative side.

- **Doodle:** Doodling can help keep us engaged when we want to zone out. Try doodling during a staff meeting or professional development training when your brain wants to exit the building. Forgive your students if they're doodling during class.

- **Make something with your hands:** Try woodworking or cooking from scratch—any activity where you have to use your hands. Using your hands to create something means that you get information from all of your senses, and this can promote more creative thinking. Neuroscientist Kelly Lambert says that "when we engage in activities, we change the neurochemistry of our brain" (as cited in Wall, 2018). Encourage your students to do the same by allowing hands-on activities and projects in class.

- **Set aside time for brainstorming:** Like anything else, creativity takes practice, so it can be helpful to set aside specific time to generate new ideas. Allow yourself some space to reflect on an area of interest or concern, and then jot down all the ideas that you come up—without editing or limiting yourself. You might use your inspiration notebook from week fourteen (page 61) for this.

- **Socialize with different people:** When we interact with people who think differently than we do, we begin to see the world in a new way. Stay open to different ways of thinking by getting to know the neighbors or colleagues you don't typically interact with. When we're at work, we usually spend the most time with our grade-level or content-area colleagues; push yourself to eat lunch with someone new, and work to really get to know that person.

- **Walk—outside in nature if you can:** Physical movement helps reduce stress, and walking in nature can be inspirational. Leave your phone in your pocket, and allow your mind to wander as you move. You might make sure your inspiration notebook is within reach, though.

Reflect on the Week

When and how did you incorporate creativity into your schedule this week? Which options did you choose and why?

....

....

How does creativity show up for you? Do you consider yourself a creative person? Why or why not?

....

....

Who is your role model or inspiration for creativity, and what can you learn from that person?

....

....

Do you plan to continue to make creativity part of your routine? Why and how?

....

....

Week Twenty: Altruism (Days 96–100)

When we recognize that someone has provided us with kindness, we should work to pay that kindness forward because "when we pay it forward we commit an act of selflessness that transcends our connection to other humans on the planet, elevating the human experience in a positive way" (Salcius, n.d.). An actual Pay it Forward Day (http://payitforwardday.com) occurs on April 28, but there's no reason we couldn't engage in this any day of the year. If this concept feels familiar, it should. In week six (page 29), the theme was altruism; I invited you to start spreading kindness throughout your day. This week is a variation on that same theme because doing something for someone else is such a massive happiness booster that it's worth circling back to this idea in a slightly different way. Consider looking back through your gratitude journal from week twelve (page 55) to see who you might pay it forward to.

 This week's invitation: Pay attention to when someone is kind to you, and then pay that kindness forward.

- **Commit to paying kindness forward:** If someone holds the door open for you, do the same for someone else. If someone smiles at you, smile at someone else. If someone offers a compliment, offer someone else a sincere compliment.

- **Count it up:** Tally how many times you were able to pay it forward each day.

Reflect on the Week

When and how did you incorporate paying it forward into your schedule this week. Which options did you choose and why?

....

....

Which actions were your favorite and why?

....

....

How did noticing others' acts of kindness make you feel?

....

....

Do you plan to continue to make paying it forward part of your routine? Why and how?

....

....

Week Twenty-One: Indulgence (Days 101–105)

I absolutely love the show *Parks and Recreation* (Yang & McDougall, 2011), and one of my all-time favorite episodes is when Donna and Tom celebrate October 13 as Treat Yo' Self day, engaging in total self-care all day long, justifying every decision with that glorious mantra *Treat. Yo. Self.* They buy themselves gifts, take the day off from their typical obligations, and eat delicious food. Brilliant. Many people have latched onto celebrating October 13 as the official Treat Yo' Self day but again, why should we limit ourselves to this one specific day of pure pleasure?

Treating yourself is as amazing as it sounds. Sure, you might not be able to step away from *all* of your obligations, and you don't want to totally lose control of your healthy habits (or credit card), but there is definitely a time and place to reward yourself, and that's exactly what this amazing week is all about! Give yourself permission to do this without any guilt! (Repeat the mantra every time you indulge; it feels so good to say it.)

 This week's invitation: Say it with me—treat yo' self.

- Stay in if you don't feel like going out.

- Go out if you don't feel like staying in.

- Take a big, fat nap.

- Buy the thing.

- Order dessert first.

- Order dessert and only dessert.

- Wear fuzzy socks or cozy slippers.

- Don't count calories.

- Take a sick day.

- Skip the shower.

- Don't answer emails, texts, or return phone calls for 24 hours.

- Get the fancy cheese and expensive crackers.

- Light the candles.

- Start a wish list on Amazon or create a new board on Pinterest.

- Partake in a spa day or visit the local brewery.

- Give into your sweet (or salty) tooth.

- Color.

- Cook or bake or make something with your hands.

- Have a dance party!

Reflect on the Week

When and how did you incorporate treating yo' self into your schedule this week? Did you pick one single day or spread your delicious self-indulgence over multiple days, and what influenced this choice?

....

....

Which treats were your favorite and why?

....

....

How did it feel to splurge or engage in activities that you normally don't do?

....

....

Do you plan to continue to make treating yourself while maintaining your overall (health, fiscal, or other) goals part of your routine? Why and how?

....

....

Week Twenty-Two: Adventure (Days 106–110)

For most of us, our days can become somewhat monotonous. We get stuck in our routines. I know it's easy for me to spend most days when I'm at home the same way: I wake up and take my dog for a long walk, I eat breakfast and settle into work for the day, I hit the gym in the late afternoon, and then I spend the evening reading before I go to bed. I love this routine and it works for me, but every once in a while, it's nice to shake things up. I want to make sure I'm having at least one adventure every single month if at all possible. Adventures for me include exploring Denver (my city) like a tourist, trying a new hiking path in the foothills, scuba diving while on vacation, and checking out the unique sites in cities that I visit for work.

 This week's invitation: Break up the monotony.

- **Make time:** Choose the day, half day, hour, or other time for your adventure, and block it out on your calendar right now.

- **Choose your adventure:** Do you want to explore a new city, store, restaurant, park, book, or topic? Start a list of adventures that sound good to you.

- **Pick your company:** Decide if you want to adventure alone or with someone else. Even going against your nature on this might be a form of adventure.

- **Do your homework:** Do the necessary research *before* your designated time. Know your route, the hours of operation, predicted forecast, and so on, so you can enjoy your adventure to the fullest.

- **Commit:** Go all in. Give yourself permission to engage in your adventure without distractions, including social media or calling into work meetings.

- **Remember:** Take one photo to record your adventure. Start an adventure photo album to capture all of your escapades and inspire yourself to make this a healthy habit!

Reflect on the Week

When and how did you incorporate an adventure into your schedule this week; what adventure did you choose and why?

....

....

How difficult was it to find time to have an adventure; did it feel like enough time?

....

....

How does adventure fit into your daily life?

....

....

Do you plan to continue to make adventure part of your routine? Why and how?

....

....

Week Twenty-Three: Orderliness (Days 111–115)

According to bestselling author Gretchen Rubin (2014), "For most people, an orderly environment helps them feel more energetic, more creative, and more cheerful." Does this feel true for you? I know this is absolutely true for me. Marie Kondō (2014), who wrote the bestselling book *The Life-Changing Magic of Tidying Up: The Japanese Art of Decluttering and Organizing*, has her own show, and was named one of *Time*'s most influential people in 2015, would no doubt agree with this sentiment.

When my desk or office is a mess, I have a hard time concentrating on tasks. I can tell that things are getting out of control for my husband and I when our house starts to fill with clutter. When I notice the mess and reflect on the various areas of my life, I can typically make a connection between the mess in one area and the mess in another area.

To help us keep a handle on our outer environments, we're going to tackle one very small strategy this week: the strategy is the one-minute rule. Here's how it works: if you can do it in one minute or less, you *must* do it (Rubin, 2006). Period. That means hanging up the coat, putting the shoes away in the closet, sorting through the mail, filing a paper, replacing the toilet paper roll, putting the dish in the dishwasher, or putting the book back on the shelf. At work, that means clearing off your desk, watering the plants, and cleaning up the coffee mugs before leaving for the day.

Consider how committing to the one-minute rule contributes to a sense of outer order but inner calm. When we take time to put things in their places, we reduce the possibility of creating or increasing visual and mental clutter.

 This week's invitation: Employ the one-minute rule.

You have one challenge this week and one challenge only: employ the one-minute rule. If you can accomplish a task in one minute or less, you must do it.

Reflect on the Week

When and how did you incorporate the one-minute rule into your schedule this week? Which options did you choose and why?

....

....

Did implementing the one-minute rule contribute to your sense of calm? How?

....

....

How do you stay on top of your clutter both at school and at home?

....

....

Do you plan to continue to make the one-minute rule part of your routine? Why and how?

....

....

Week Twenty-Four: Obligations (Days 116–120)

I listen to the podcast *Happier in Hollywood* (2018; http://happierinhollywood.com) every single week. While I don't live in Hollywood (Denver is a far cry from Tinseltown), I still love Liz Craft and Sarah Fain's tips, suggestions, and hacks regarding ways to bring even more happiness to my daily life—particularly my professional life. In episode 71, the hosts challenge listeners to take an *obligation vacation* based on Sarah's own experiment (http://happierinhollywood.com/episode71).

I immediately connected to this challenge and found myself considering things that I could take a break from for a day or two without suffering huge ramifications. For example, I opted to not make the bed, opted out of cleaning my office that week, and let my laundry go longer than I usually do. It was so freeing! I knew that I wouldn't lose the habit by only opting out for a short time and that life does indeed go on if the bed isn't made and my home office is messy.

 This week's invitation: Consider the obligations that you could use a small vacation from, and then grant yourself permission to do that.

You can skip these house obligations (for at least a while).

- Cooking dinner
- Making the bed
- Washing the laundry
- Folding the laundry
- Ironing the laundry
- Going to the gym
- Planning meals
- Going grocery shopping

Try not doing these work obligations on days when you *can't even* (even if only for 24 hours).

- Grading papers
- Planning next week's lesson
- Tidying the classroom
- Cleaning your desk
- Updating your website
- Checking your voicemail
- Answering every email

You can get away without doing these social obligations for a while.

- Responding to friends' texts or emails

- Returning calls

- Meeting for drinks or dinner

- Replying to comments people have made to you on social media

Reflect on the Week

When and how did you incorporate an obligation vacation into your schedule this week? Which option did you choose and why?

....

....

How did it feel to take an obligation vacation, and did anything suffer as a result?

....

....

Was your obligation vacation difficult to follow through on? Why or why not?

....

....

Do you plan to continue to make obligation vacations part of your routine? Why and how?

....

....

Week Twenty-Five: Play (Days 121–125)

Playtime isn't just for kids. Adults need to play, too! Just because we're all grown up now doesn't mean that we can't still have some fun simply for fun's sake. "Play brings joy. And it's vital for problem solving, creativity, and relationships" (Tartakovsky, 2018). As adults, it can feel indulgent or a bit silly to play, but this week you're going to crush that way of thinking, because the truth is, "if we want to live a life of meaning and contribution, we have to become intentional about cultivating sleep and play" (Brown, 2018, p. 106).

Pause for a moment and consider what play meant to you when you were a child. What did you do when you were playing? Who did you have playdates with? What were your favorite toys? What did your imagination dream up when you had moments of boredom? Chances are, some of those notions might still appeal to you today, as an adult, even if you've buried them due to obligations, full schedules, and a need to *adult*.

Consider how adult coloring books have made such a dramatic comeback. I used to love to color, play four square, ride my bike, and create (I could spend hours cutting images and words out of magazines to make collages). And guess what? I *still* love to do those things. I strive to make time for play every single week. My husband and I take long bike rides, explore a new neighborhood, or admire the art at local festivals and galleries.

This week's invitation: Have some fun.

- **Monday:** To set the tone for the week, take twenty-six minutes to watch a glorious TED Talk titled "Play Is More Than Just Fun" by Stuart Brown (2008; https://bit .ly/1e1z9LS), who pioneered research about playing. In it, Brown talks about the importance of play, which includes games, roughhousing, and fantasy. You can watch part of it in the morning and the rest in the evening, or you can divide this task between today and tomorrow and combine Tuesday's and Wednesday's invitations; they fit together nicely.

- **Tuesday:** Reflect on your own play history. What did play look like to you when you were a child? As an adolescent? As a young adult? What were your favorite playtime activities when you were alone? With friends? Which of these activities still appeal to you now? Make a list.

- **Wednesday:** Who do you play with now, as an adult? What does play look like, feel like, and sound like? Can you schedule a playdate with a friend, family member, colleague, or child? (Taking kids to the park gives you an excuse to hop on the swings!)

- **Thursday and Friday:** Go play! For these two days, do something that feels like total play to you—even if only for fifteen minutes. Ride a bike, play kickball, have a dance party in your kitchen, design your dream house or ultimate vacation, or challenge someone to a lip sync contest.

Consider ways you can play during the school day, too! After all, "if you are having a good time, chances are your students are too" (Briggs, 2015). Research confirms, too, "that fun is not just beneficial to learning but, by many reports, required for authentic learning and long-term memory" (Sean Slade, as cited in Briggs, 2015). Have a dance party, play some music, run around with students at recess, or visit them during gym class!

Reflect on the Week

When and how did you incorporate play into your schedule this week? Which options did you choose and why?

....

....

How did it feel to make time for play?

....

....

Do you prefer to play alone or with others? What did you learn about play and yourself this week, and was anything a surprise?

....

....

Do you plan to continue to make play part of your routine? Why and how?

....

....

Week Twenty-Six: Email (Days 126–130)

Have you seen the meme about how there are two different types of people in the world—those with thousands of emails in their inbox and those who can't rest until they're at zero? Whether you fall distinctly into one of these categories or you're somewhere in between, this week is about managing your inbox and your sanity at the same time.

How do your inboxes (work and personal) make you feel? Does email feel like a burden? Does it feel overwhelming? Does it make you feel stressed out? Those messages can take on a life of their own, and rather than you being the boss, it can feel like the inbox controls your life.

Consider the following information: the average person checks email 566 times a day (Zomorodi, 2017). Now, consider that "shifting between tasks can cost as much as 40 percent of someone's productive time" (David Meyer, as cited in American Psychological Association, 2006). Personally, I'm an inbox zero kind of gal, and because of that, seeing the notifications of unopened emails became an obsession—something I needed to deal with immediately. I'm embarrassed to admit this, but for a long time I felt an urgency to *immediately* respond to any email that came in, whether I was at the grocery store, asleep, or even— *yikes*—on vacation. As I worked to make significant changes in my life to increase my overall happiness and well-being, learning how to make email work *for* me rather than *against* me was a hurdle I had to tackle.

Today, I am in control of my email, not the other way around. I check my email at scheduled times throughout the day, I choose when to respond rather than imposing an artificial and unhealthy deadline of *immediately*, and I allow myself to be fully present in whatever moment I'm in (be it the grocery store, my reading chair, or vacation). It's OK if I don't respond to an email within minutes of its arrival into my inbox. I allow myself a twenty-four-hour rule during the workweek and a seventy-two-hour rule on the weekend. It's glorious and freeing.

This week's invitation: Rethink your relationship with email.

- **Monday:** Conduct a self-audit to determine how many times a day you check your email. Like you did with social media, just taking a tally on a sticky note will do. Consider how you feel about the results, if you'd like to lower this number, and why (Raphael, 2017).

- **Tuesday:** Consider how you can be the boss of your email rather than allowing your email to be the boss of you. Can you schedule time in your day for checking and responding to emails rather than checking it nonstop throughout the day? What if you take twenty focused minutes two or three times a day to check your email (Ericson, 2014)?

- **Wednesday:** Check in on your email habits (Raphael, 2017). Can you think about your email more like a text so that your responses are shorter and more direct? Can you keep common sentence starters, pleasantries, and closings on your clipboard so you can copy and paste rather than retyping each time you start a new email?

- **Thursday:** Get rid of it! Use the website unroll.me (https://unroll.me) to clean out the junk! This (amazing) service allows you to sort through every list you're subscribed to and decide if you want to keep it in your inbox, unsubscribe from it, or *roll it up*. For the emails that you choose to roll up, you'll receive one email per day (you choose if you want to receive that email in the morning, afternoon, or evening) that contains everything you want to keep but perhaps don't want flooding your inbox. This service also continually monitors your emails and lets you know when it finds any new subscriptions so you can again choose to keep, delete, or roll up. It's life changing. Seriously.

  You might consider using a so-called *burner* email address dedicated to when you sign up for something or purchase something online. That way, subsequent subscription emails go there, staying separate from your important messages at your other email address.

- **Friday:** Stop with the folders (unless this works for you, of course). For most of us, attempting to drag emails into designated folders is just one more step that backfires. It can be difficult to find what you're looking for when you need it if it's buried in a folder. Instead, use the flag, unread, and pinned features and simply search by date, content, or sender to find what you need.

Reflect on the Week

When and how did you incorporate taking control of your email this week? Which options did you choose and why?

....

....

How did it feel to take control of your inbox, and in doing so, what did you learn about your email habits this week? Did anything surprise you?

....

....

Could you apply some of these same principles to your texts, tweets, or social media messages? How and why might doing this increase your happiness and well-being?

....

....

Do you plan to continue to make keeping your email habits in check part of your routine?

....

....

Week Twenty-Seven: Replay (Days 131–135)

I learned about this week's habit and all the powerful research behind it and decided to give it a try (Pasricha, 2016). I found it is a game changer. The twenty-minute replay (or even the five-minute replay) asks you to write for twenty minutes (or five minutes or ten minutes or whatever you can find time for) about a positive experience you've had. The research shows that this replay writing *dramatically* improves happiness because your brain relives that experience while you're writing about and then rereading it (Pasricha, 2016).

I started writing—in detail—about something positive that took place in the last twenty-four hours. It's sloppy and imperfect and isn't formal like an essay; it's more like bullet points of the details—but it works. I am able to feel, at my desk, those wonderful feelings that I felt when I was actually living them. I find myself writing quickly and passionately because I'm *there* (in my mind) and want to hold on to that feeling for as long as I can. I also spend time at the end of the week rereading my reflections, thus allowing one more opportunity to flood my brain with these powerful moments.

 This week's invitation: Write about the good stuff.

1. Schedule between five and twenty minutes of quiet time during your day. Perhaps you want to experiment with different times to see if the morning is better for you than the afternoon, or if the evening seems to be your sweet spot.

2. Record the best moments. Consider where you were, who you were with, what someone said or did, how you felt, and why this moment was such a highlight. Bonus! You're likely to experience gratitude as you do this, and we know that gratitude is a powerful thing. See week twelve (page 55).

You might consider doing this activity with students, too. If you don't have a full twenty minutes, you could still lead them through a five-minute version of this activity so they can reap the benefits as well.

Woohoo! You just wrapped up another nine weeks and are officially three-quarters of the way done with your invitations! Again, I want you to pause here to think back over the previous nine weeks. Highlight, on the Notes page (page 103), which invitations and options worked for you, which need more time, and how you're feeling at this point in your journey. And above all else, keep going! You're doing an amazing job.

Reflect on the Week

When and how did you incorporate replay writing into your schedule this week? Did you also find time to do this with students? How did they like it?

....

....

How did writing about good experiences make you feel? How did reading what you wrote later on make you feel, and did you feel differently in each case?

....

....

Did five minutes of writing feel long or short; how about twenty minutes? What is the sweet spot for your writing time and why?

....

....

Do you plan to continue to make replaying the best part of your day part of your routine? Why and how?

....

....

·NOTES·

CHAPTER 4

Finishing Strong

Ending the calendar year strong rather than exhausted, depressed, and bloated greatly appeals to me, and so I work extra hard to stay conscious of my choices during October, November, and December. The same can be done with the school year and this work we're doing for ourselves. Challenge yourself to *fully* commit to the next nine weeks' worth of invitations without breaking promises to yourself. Write reminders on sticky notes to keep yourself going and to cheer yourself on.

Because the end of the school year can get chaotic, it's even *more* essential that you engage in this work and take time every week to incorporate these invitations. You can do this. I *know* you can do this. *You* know you can do it, too. You wouldn't break a promise to a loved one, so decide that you're not going to break a promise to yourself, either. This year you're going to finish strong by taking care of yourself and bringing your best energy to school!

Now, press Play on your go-to good-mood playlist, jump around or move your body to get yourself pumped up, and get fired up to finish this year strong and *fierce*!

Week Twenty-Eight: Hobbies (Days 136–140)

Because so many of us are somewhat (if not completely) addicted to devices and Netflix, we've lost the art of the hobby. According to psychology professor Jaime L. Kurtz (2015), hobbies allow us to structure our time, help with stress, foster new social connections, and make us more interesting! Do you have a hobby? Did you used to enjoy a hobby but lost it in the hustle and bustle of your daily routine? Do you *wish* you had a hobby? This week you're celebrating the hobbies that you have or starting a new hobby.

One of my favorite hobbies is reading. I take such immense pleasure in the written word, and I like to read multiple books at the same time (usually one novel, one professional book, and a personal growth book). I've always loved to read and always make time for it, but for a few years, I read significantly less than I do now. Once I regained control of my habits around social media, Netflix, and other distractions, I read more than I ever had before, and I was so grateful to have reclaimed this hobby.

As you get ready to take this invitation, think about hobbies you already have or once had. How did you discover the things you love doing?

 This week's invitation: Try a new hobby or enjoy an established hobby.

- **Monday:** If you *do* have a hobby, reflect on how much time you currently devote to that hobby. Is this enough? Would you like to find more time? If you *don't* have a hobby, start a list of all the things that interest you and what your hobbies used to be. Choose something that you want to pursue; make sure it's something that excites you, not something that you feel obligated to do. Some unique ideas include things like bonsai, geocaching, dancing (ballroom, hip hop, line-dancing), fencing, and origami.

- **Tuesday:** Schedule time in your calendar to engage in your hobby. Decide if you want to do this daily, biweekly, or weekly, and then block out time for yourself— without guilt.

- **Wednesday through Friday:** Get to it! Stick to your commitment, turn off your devices, and allow yourself the gift of absorbing yourself in your hobby fully. Set a timer if it's important that you have a start and end time.

Reflect on the Week

When and how did you incorporate your hobby into your schedule this week?
Did you do each part of the activity option? Why or why not?

....

....

How did it feel to schedule time (or *more* time) for your hobby?

....

....

Were you able to fully engage in your hobby, or did you feel distracted? How can
you give yourself the gift of full presence while you engage in your hobby?

....

....

Do you plan to continue to make your hobby part of your routine, or to keep
looking for one you enjoy?

....

....

Week Twenty-Nine: Cognition (Days 141–145)

By engaging in activities that keep your mind sharp, you're better able to deal with the problems and challenges that life invariably throws at you. In fact, "if you maintain the attitude that stress is a challenge—rather than a threat, you are better able to handle it" (Scott, 2018). The type of learning that you're going to focus on this week has nothing to do with grades or external competition; instead, you're going to play around with options that will sharpen your mind.

Setting up opportunities for our brains to work hard, persevere, and problem solve can ward off dementia and Alzheimer's disease (Tennstedt & Unverzagt, 2013). I love a good (but easy) crossword puzzle—hello, *People Magazine*—and solitaire game and have many friends who swear by the joy that Sudoku puzzles bring them. The benefit is in the challenge, the presence and focus, and the feeling of accomplishment when we win, finish, or even just get through most of it. (The options that follow are adapted from Smith, Robinson, & Segal, 2019).

 This week's invitation: Build your brain muscles.

- **Learn something new:** Learning new things helps our brains stay sharp (Park et al., 2014). Learn to garden, try orienteering, or ride a tandem bicycle with a friend. Prefer quieter activities and already know how to knit? Consider embroidery, weaving, or felting. Woodworking projects might be fun. If you usually read fiction, read a nonfiction article or book, or vice versa. Or consider choosing a book that is set in a place or time period that you would like to learn more about. *I Am Malala: The Girl Who Stood Up for Education and Was Shot by the Taliban* (Yousafzai, 2013) and *A Long Way Gone: Memoirs of a Boy Soldier* (Beah, 2007) are just two examples of novels that address experiences everyone can relate to—growing up, the complexities of family life, and loss—but each is tied distinctly to a particular time, place, and set of cultural pressures. You might sign up for a book discussion group at your library or take a class at a local fiber arts store, community center, or adult education center. Once you choose something new to learn, practice that new thing regularly. The greater the novelty, complexity, and challenge, the greater the benefit for your brain.

- **Get better at something you already know how to do:** Perhaps now is not the time to learn something entirely new. Instead, challenge your brain by increasing your skills and knowledge of something you already do. For example, if you play guitar and don't want to switch to a new instrument, commit to learning a new piece of music. If you usually play solo, you could try making music with a group instead. If you're a swimmer, fine-tune your forward crawl and beat that eighty-six second one hundred-meter personal best!

- **Memorize information:** Start with something short and then work your way up to something longer or more challenging if you like this invitation. You can utilize rhymes and word associations to strengthen your memory connections (Dove, n.d.).

- **Enjoy strategy games and puzzles:** Spend some time working on a crossword puzzle or playing a board game, card game, or word and number games such as Scrabble or mancala. There are apps for these games if you don't have the tangible versions.

- **Practice the five Ws:** Think like a journalist or a detective, and record a five W—*who, what, when, where,* and *why*—list of your daily experiences (Smith et al., 2019). Capturing these visual details keeps your neurons firing. Your list can be as simple as this one.

  - *Who*—My husband
  - *What*—Dinner out
  - *When*—April 16
  - *Where*—Sarto's
  - *Why*—Because neither of us wanted to cook tonight—what a treat!

- **Follow the road less traveled:** Take a new route to work, experiment with eating or brushing your teeth using your nondominant hand, or try parting your hair on the opposite side. Varying your habits in this way creates new brain pathways (Smith et al., 2019).

Reflect on the Week

When and how did you incorporate building your brain muscles into your schedule this week? Which options did you choose and why?

....

....

Did you discover a new potential passion or hobby this week?

....

....

Were you able to fully engage with your brain building, or did this invitation not work for you?

....

....

How can you continue to make keeping your brain sharp part of your routine?

....

....

Week Thirty: Transitions (Days 146–150)

Moving from one task, event, or mindset to another can be tough, and yet, as educators, we're tasked with this challenge all day, every day. In fact, "every day, people lose tremendous amounts of focus, will, and emotional energy by managing transitions poorly" (Burchard, 2017, p. 98). This week you're going to engage in the intentional practice of learning how to manage transitions. When I read about this practice in Brendon Burchard's (2017) book *High Performance Habits*, I implemented it immediately, and the results astounded me. Being mindful of each transition during my day revitalized my life, and that is not an exaggeration.

I know that one of my most difficult transitions comes when I finish conducting a workshop. Because my adrenaline is pumping and my heart rate is up for hours during a training, I crash hard once I say goodbye to the participants and get into my rental car. Because I had no technique for closing out that part of my day and moving into my evening, I was making choices that were not aligned to my overall goals, particularly my health and happiness goals. I often arrived at the airport with insatiable hunger, and I easily gave in to temptations and ordered french fries without a second thought only to regret my choice just minutes after finishing my plate. I was snippy with TSA agents and the general public, and this frustrated me immensely because treating people with respect and kindness is a core value for me. When I learned how to master this major transition (and other minor transitions throughout my entire day) using the technique that I'm about to show you, I was able to stay aligned to my core values and my personal commitments to my overall health and well-being.

As you get ready to take this week's invitation, begin thinking about the transitions that you go through during your day. The following options are adapted from Burchard (2017).

 This week's invitation: Manage transitions.

- **Consider your typical transitions:** Do some thinking about your transitions. Find a sheet of paper, or open a Word document on your computer. Write down what your typical daily and weekly transitions are. Going to

work and coming home will likely show up on your
list. What about transitions at school? These can be
particularly difficult: students moving from activity to
activity or class to class can be disruptive. What about
moving from a day of school to meetings? Additionally, in
the school setting, you must not only manage transitions
for yourself but help students manage them as well.

....

....

....

- **Reflect on transitions, extend understanding, and
  respond:** After recording your regular transitions,
  reflect and write on the following questions about your
  transitions (Bhavsar, 2017, p. 335):

    o Which transitions are hardest for you, and what
      do you think makes them so hard? Do you have
      any transitions that feel like a breeze; why might
      this be so?

    o Do you ever carry over any negative energy from
      one activity to the next?

    o Do you ever feel depleted but still plow into your
      next activity without a break, even though you
      know you should take a breather?

    o Are you losing a sense of presence and
      appreciation for life and others the further you go
      in your day?

  Now, save these written reflections on your typical
  transitions and reflect on larger transitions in your life.
  Have you moved to a new house recently? Adopted a new
  pet? Has your child left home for college? How might
  your larger life transitions be influencing your typical
  daily and weekly transitions? For instance, does disruptive
  and rowdy behavior by your students strike a painful cord
  with you lately because you miss your own child, even
  his or her crazy behavior? How might you respond to

awareness about larger life transitions that may be making your typical daily and weekly transitions difficult for you?

- **Extend response to transition:** Sometimes a simple awareness of cause and effect can help you reduce stress from a transition, and sometimes you need to add meaningful steps to your routine to calm yourself. As you finish one major activity and start another, consider following these three steps (Bhavsar, 2017):

  a. Close your eyes for one or two minutes.

  b. Repeat the word *release* in your mind over and over and over. As you do this, command your body to let go by relaxing your shoulders, neck, face, and jaw. Keep repeating *release* as you do this. When you feel like you've released some tension (it doesn't have to be *all* of it), move to step three.

  c. Set an intention. How do you want to feel? What do you want to accomplish in the next activity? Ask yourself what energy you want to take into the next activity.

  Practice this three-step process deliberately and intentionally every single day this week.

- **Assist your students through transitions:** Speak to your students about transitions in their days. Which ones are hardest for them and why? Which ones are hard for you? You might have kindergarteners sit in a circle and each draw a picture of their favorite part of the day, share their pictures, and then guide a conversation with them about why it is both hard but necessary to transition to the next activity. Can you end class one or two minutes early and invite high school students to practice Aditya Bhavsar's (2017) calming techniques with you? They might roll their eyes at first, but chances are, they will find some value in the practice of consciously releasing a moment before moving on to something else.

Reflect on the Week

When and how did you incorporate managing your transitions into your schedule this week? Which options, or parts of an option, did you choose and why?

....

....

Did managing your transitions help you better deal with stress and be more in the moment? How?

....

....

What else did you learn from managing transitions or helping your students manage their transitions, and did you notice a change in those around you—your students, your family?

....

....

Do you plan to continue making managing your transitions part of your daily routine? Why and how? Are there other transitions that you'd like to continue to work on?

....

....

Week Thirty-One: Listening (Days 151–155)

In this age of technology and communication via texts and emojis, I fear that we're starting to lose the art of *listening like heaven* when we're engaged in face-to-face conversation. Consider the last time that you felt really and truly *heard*. What a gift that is. (Hence, the phrase *listening like heaven*.) When someone puts their technology away, looks you in the eye, leans in, and nods and smiles instead of interrupting, that makes you feel as though you are the most important person in the entire world. That? That is an incredible gift. Rachel Naomi Remen (2006) says the "most basic and powerful way to connect to another person is to listen. Just listen. Perhaps the most important thing we ever give each other is our attention" (p. 112).

When I'm out with friends or family members, I make a conscious effort to keep my phone away from the table, and I make it my entire goal to be the very best listener that I can possibly be. I work hard to listen without interrupting with my own stories (this is difficult for me), I try to ask thoughtful questions, and I always express gratitude for what someone has shared with me. My relationships feel stronger than ever these days, and that's so important to me.

 This week's invitation: Just listen.

- **Connect with a peer:** Choose at least one colleague or friend to connect with, and schedule a coffee (or dinner or lunch or a walk) date for some time this week. While you're with that person, provide the gift of listening like heaven. Beforehand, think of some open-ended questions that you legitimately want to know about the person.

  Who will you connect with this week?

  ....

  Record the open-ended questions that you will ask to get the conversation started.

  ....

  ....

- **Connect with a student:** Choose at least one student to connect with, and schedule a time to talk (perhaps during lunch or recess or before or after school). While you're with that student, provide the gift of listening like heaven. Beforehand, think of some open-ended questions that you're legitimately interested in learning about from this student.

  Which student will you connect with this week?

  ....

  Record the open-ended questions that you will ask to get the conversation started.

  ....

  ....

Reflect on the Week

When and how did you incorporate attentive listening into your schedule this week? Who did you give your full attention to and why?

....

....

What were your conscious behaviors as you listened like heaven? Did you notice anything different when you were talking with a peer versus a student?

....

....

How did it feel to provide this gift to someone you care about? Was it helpful to plan your open-ended questions ahead of time? How often did you find yourself fighting the urge to interrupt?

....

....

Do you plan to continue to make attentive listening part of your routine? Why and how?

....

....

Week Thirty-Two: Journal (Days 156–160)

I've written in a journal for as long as I can remember. It's how I process challenges, where I record my daily gratitude statements and intentions, and where I jot down new ideas, favorite quotes, twenty-minute replays, frustrations, and funny memories. Journaling grounds me and helps me manage stress and anxiety, and there's research that tells me that I'm not alone. James Pennebaker, psychologist and researcher, explains that "writing about stressful events helps you come to terms with them, acting as a stress management tool, thus reducing the impact of these stressors on your physical health" (Purcell, 2018). It also helps us manage anxiety and depression (University of Rochester Medical Center, n.d.).

Even if you don't consider yourself a writer, journaling can still be beneficial. Scientific evidence points out these additional benefits to journaling: it can clarify what you're thinking and feeling, it helps you to know yourself better, it can reduce stress, it can help you solve problems more effectively, and it can be a tool to help you resolve disagreements with others more easily. Don't worry about spelling, punctuation, or grammar. Journaling isn't like writing an essay or an assignment; it's about getting your thoughts out of your mind. All you need is something to write in, something to write with (on paper or electronically), some time alone, and a willingness to let go and just write. (The following options are from University of Rochester Medical Center, n.d.).

This week's invitation: Just write.

- **Schedule a time to write, and try to write every day:** Set aside a specific time to write in your journal each day. Can you do a few minutes in the morning? What about during lunch break, or before bed? Be intentional about your time, think of it as a gift to yourself, and then use that time to write!

- **Set the stage:** Select a notebook for your journal that you feel comfortable with. Would you like something with a colorful cover or a hand-bound journal made from homemade paper? Perhaps you want a simple, nondescript spiral-bound notebook. Once you have your journal notebook, keep it handy along with a pen so that when you want to jot down your thoughts, you can. You can also keep a journal in a computer file. If you have a portable device, you may still access your journal any time.

- **Write whatever feels right:** Your journal doesn't need to follow any particular structure, but it can. Experiment with different modes of writing. Write only about what you see in the natural world one day, write about your dreams, or brainstorm about ways you could solve a problem that currently occupies you. Or, let the words flow freely without worrying about spelling mistakes or what other people might think. It's your own private arena to discuss whatever you want.

- **Use your journal as you see fit:** You don't have to share your journal with anyone, but if you discover that you like what you've written, consider turning your writing into an article, letter, or blog post. If you do want to share some of your thoughts with trusted friends and loved ones but don't want to talk about them out loud, you could show them parts of your journal.

Reflect on the Week

When and how did you incorporate journaling into your schedule this week?
Which options did you choose and why?

....

....

How often did you journal this week and for how long each time? What were the
challenges of taking time to journal, or of journaling itself?

....

....

How did it feel to journal, and how did journaling benefit you, both as an
educator and personally?

....

....

Do you plan to continue to make journaling part of your routine? Why and how?

....

....

Week Thirty-Three: Outdoors (Days 161–165)

What if there were a miracle drug that could relieve stress almost instantly—would you take it? What if I said you don't even need to pop a pill; all you need to do is step outside? Fantastic, right? This week you're getting yourself outside. That's it. Go to a park or a forest or your backyard or the playground.

According to Florence Williams (2017) in her fascinating book *The Nature Fix: Why Nature Makes Us Happier, Healthier, and More Creative*, when we're stuck indoors, we're actually harming our mental and physical health. Instead, we should remember this: the more nature that we feel and experience, the better we'll feel. That's it. Even as little as fifteen minutes in the woods reduces the stress hormone cortisol. If you've got forty-five minutes for nature, you'll experience cognitive improvements, too (Mark, 2017).

Being in nature can also help us feel connected to something greater than ourselves, and that need is at the very top of our self-care ladders (and Maslow's Hierarchy of Needs; Boogren, 2018). When we're able to gaze at the wonders of the outside world, we are filled with that incredible emotion of awe.

I'm lucky enough to live in the beautiful state of Colorado, and I make a deliberate effort to get outside as often as possible. Through blazing sun, howling wind, and soft snow, my goal is to take our dog, Harry, on a walk outside every single morning that I'm home. Between those morning walks with my dog, hiking in the foothills, biking the tremendous trails nestled throughout the city and in the mountains, I'd much rather get my endorphins going out in nature rather than being stuck in the gym (although I've logged a lot of miles that way, too, when the weather is particularly brutal). When I'm outside, I try to keep my phone tucked away, and I rarely use my headphones. I strive to engage all of my senses in the experience, especially my hearing. I absolutely love breathing in the fresh mountain air, feeling the sun (or wind or rain or snow) on my face, and disconnecting from my other obligations for a while. This week is about stepping outside and savoring the great outdoors—whether that means your lawn, a city park, or a country road.

This week's invitation: Get outside for at least fifteen minutes every day this week.

- **Walk:** Take a walk in the morning, during your lunch hour, or after school. Leave all of your devices behind (but please consider your safety). Walk by yourself or grab a walking buddy (especially a four-legged one). Maybe slip your shoes off if you can.

- **Rest:** Sit in the grass against a tree or simply lie down. How does resting outside feel?

- **Eat:** Take your morning coffee outside or eat a meal outside, picnic-style.

- **Notice:** Keep your eyes open and notice the minute details all around you. Then try closing your eyes in order to engage your other senses. What do you hear, feel, and smell all around you?

- **Breathe:** Take some deep belly breaths. You can look back at week nine (page 38) for a refresher on how to do this.

- **Take your students outside:** Can you teach outside for a bit? Or take a five-minute walk as a brain break? What do you notice about your students when you're able to get outside of the classroom for a bit?

- **Experiment:** Experiment with parks, forests, beaches, mountains, and country roads (depending on where you live). Do you enjoy going somewhere close, or do you like to get in your car and drive to another location?

Reflect on the Week

When and how did you incorporate getting outside this week? Which options did you choose and why?

....

....

What did you discover about yourself and your relationship with nature? How did being out in nature make you feel?

....

....

What were the challenges and benefits of getting outside?

....

....

Do you plan to continue to make daily or weekly outdoor time part of your routine? Why and how?

....

....

Week Thirty-Four: Morning Routine (Days 166–170)

What does your morning routine currently look like? How do you feel in the morning? What are your morning challenges? What do you wish you could change about your morning routine? For many of us, mornings are particularly challenging. It's difficult to get out of bed, the to-do list is overwhelming, and other people (children, spouses, and even animals) need us and can derail us. The challenges go on and on.

I used to absolutely loathe the morning. In general, I'm not what you'd call a morning person. My husband will vouch for my crabbiness for the first thirty minutes or so after my getting up. That crabbiness hasn't gone away, but I've learned to redirect it and allow myself the gift of time in the morning so that I can enter my day calm and centered rather than feeling rushed and rattled. Here's how I do it: I allow myself *at least* two full hours between when my alarm goes off and getting out the door to wherever I need to be in the morning.

I know, I know—two full hours might sound ridiculous, but it's what works for me, and "how you start your day has a great impact on your attitude and achievements all day long" (Pierce, 2013). When I have this much time, I'm able to engage in the routines and habits that are essential for me to get my day going on the right foot. I move my body (either a quick walk or stretching or yoga), I write my gratitude list and my intentions in my journal, I chug my water before diving headfirst into my coffee, and I meditate. These are my daily four commitments for the morning—(1) move, (2) write, (3) chug, and (4) meditate—and I've worked hard to build muscle memory around these so I don't even have to think about them; I just do them.

A good morning routine usually comes from a well thought-out evening routine, so also consider what steps you can take the night before to set yourself up for success in the morning. The options in week three (page 20) can help streamline your evening routine.

This week's invitation: Make over your morning.

- **Start small:** You can plan your mornings. Decide what small thing you'd like to make time for in the morning, decide how long that action will take, and set your alarm accordingly. Perhaps you want to start with just getting up ten minutes earlier on Monday so you can drink your coffee on the couch by yourself, or maybe you want to allow ten minutes to make your lunch for the day.

- **Build from there:** You can build from there as the week goes on (ultimately getting up twenty-five to thirty minutes earlier than usual), making time to watch an inspiring video, take a walk, practice deep breathing, or read for pleasure.

Reflect on the Week

How did you incorporate making over your morning into your schedule this week? Which options did you choose and why?

....

....

What was your favorite change to your morning (or evening) routine this week?

....

....

What were the challenges and benefits of rethinking your morning routine?

....

....

Do you plan to continue this morning (or evening) routine? Why or why not?

....

....

Week Thirty-Five: Active Rest (Days 171–175)

While it's important to set goals and be active and hustle (in a healthy way), it's also so very important and essential to *rest*. Without guilt. So much of our time and our brain space is filled with work and to-do lists and obligations and activities and worry that we rarely allow ourselves rest.

Rest is different than sleep (although of course these two are connected; see week three, page 20, for a refresher on the importance of sleep). Rest includes slowing down *during our waking hours*. According to author Tim Kreider (2012), "Idleness is not just a vacation, an indulgence or a vice; it is as indispensable to the brain as vitamin D is to the body, and deprived of it we suffer a mental affliction as disfiguring as rickets."

Many of us have a difficult time resting. Instead, we feel a need to fill every waking moment with *something*. Trust me when I tell you that I fall into this trap often as I've always associated productivity with success and have had to work hard to allow myself to engage in idle time without feeling like I'm losing ground. If it helps, researchers Mary Helen Immordino-Yang, Joanna A. Christodoulou, and Vanessa Singh (2012) titled their study "Rest Is Not Idleness," and *Scientific American* explains that research by saying that "downtime is in fact essential to mental processes that affirm our identities, develop our understanding of human behavior and instill an internal code of ethics" (Jabr, 2013).

Because of the steps I've consciously taken to curb my addiction to my devices, I've also increased my capacity for purposeful, waking rest, or *active rest*. As someone who deals with anxiety, rest has proven to be a balm for my anxiousness, allowing me to feel calmer and more centered and thus able to tackle the next invitation more confidently.

 This week's invitation: Practice downtime and find opportunities for active rest.

- **Monday and Tuesday:** Make a conscious effort to live in the moment on both Monday and Tuesday. Here's how to do it (adapted from Miller, 2018).

- o Designate a specific time in your day to focus on what's right in front of you.

- o Bring your mind back to the present moment every time it tries to drift off. You can say to yourself, "I'll get back to worrying later."

- o Help yourself stay in the moment by asking yourself what you hear, see, taste, feel, and smell.

- **Wednesday:** Engage in mindful eating today. Try the following tips to get started (adapted from Harvard Health Publishing, 2016).

   - o Before you begin eating, take a moment or two to simply appreciate the food in front of you.

   - o Bring all of your senses to the meal. Notice the color, texture, smell, seasonings, and how the food feels in your mouth and as you swallow.

   - o Take small bites, chew thoroughly, and eat slowly (putting your utensils down between each bite).

- **Thursday and Friday:** Schedule thirty minutes of relaxation on both Thursday and Friday. You can use this window to simply sit quietly, allowing your mind to wander and rest, or you can engage in relaxing activities like the following.

   - o Savor a cup of tea (or any other nonstimulant beverage).

   - o Stare out a window.

   - o Sit outside and people watch.

   - o Reflect on what you're grateful for right now.

Reflect on the Week

When and how did you incorporate active rest into your schedule this week?
Which options did you choose and why?

....

....

What was your favorite way to rest this week and why?

....

....

How did it feel to actively rest? What were the challenges and benefits of allowing
yourself to rest this week?

....

....

Do you plan to continue to make active rest part of your routine? Why and how?

....

....

Week Thirty-Six: Summer Bucket List (Days 176–180)

For your final week (*you made it!*), you're going to create your summer bucket list. To note, it's OK if summer isn't what awaits you at the end of this week; just create a list for the next season. Finishing this book marks an end to our time together but also the start of your taking off the training wheels and putting into practice all that you've learned about yourself, and all (or some) of your new habits and practices! This list is meant to be fun and give you something additional to look forward to. Set aside a few minutes each day to add to your list.

 This week's invitation: Start your summer bucket list.

- Go for a bike ride.
- Do a cartwheel.
- Fly a kite.
- Go to a drive-in movie theater.
- Have a picnic.
- Start a water fight.
- Play in a sprinkler.
- Do a cannonball into the pool.
- Rest in a hammock.
- Buy something at a garage or estate sale.
- Eat a hot dog straight from the grill.
- Chase down the ice-cream truck (or make your own popsicles).
- Go to a farmer's market.
- Sport a temporary tattoo.
- Visit the library.
- Catch fireflies.
- Go camping.
- Jump in puddles.
- Paint something.

- Volunteer somewhere.
- Plant flowers—seeds, annuals, perennials, or vegetables.
- Travel somewhere you've never been.
- Eat breakfast for dinner.
- Spend a day barefoot.
- Go fishing.
- Enjoy a tropical drink.
- Play Frisbee, hopscotch, Wiffle Ball, or volleyball.
- Visit an amusement park.
- Attend a baseball game.

Yeeehawwww! You, my friend, have *done* it! Can you believe it? I am so proud of you! Before you move on to the epilogue, stop right now and do a little happy dance! Done? Nice! Now I'll ask you to pause again here in order to consider these past nine weeks and to reflect on what challenges made the biggest difference in your life, what you'd like to try again, and what your life feels like after these 180 days. Like before, you can record your thoughts on the Notes page on page 134.

Reflect on the Week

When and how did you incorporate making your summer bucket list into your schedule this week? What did you choose to add to your list and why?

....

....

What are you most looking forward to during your next season?

....

....

How did it feel to create your list; what, if anything, made it tough to start or complete your summer bucket list? How can you plan ahead to overcome these challenges?

....

....

How can you use a summer bucket list in another season of your life or school year? (See the epilogue, page 135, for ideas.)

....

....

·NOTES·

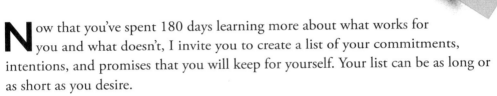

Create Your Own Self-Care List

Now that you've spent 180 days learning more about what works for you and what doesn't, I invite you to create a list of your commitments, intentions, and promises that you will keep for yourself. Your list can be as long or as short as you desire.

As we come to a close, think back on some of what you've experimented with over the past 180 days. You've taken time to think about your diet and sleep, and you've made playlists and taken adventures! You've learned how to manage transitions and spent time outside. You've tackled your social media and emails and learned how to say *no* and how to ask for help. You've employed the one-minute rule, engaged in altruistic acts, practiced gratitude, and made yourself laugh. Wow. You've been on quite a journey, and undoubtedly some weeks worked better for you than others. You may have some regrets or wish you could have a do-over in some areas. Luckily, the sky is the limit from here! You can re-engage in this work any time, in any way. Maybe you want to begin all over again with the start of the next school year. Maybe you want to revisit certain weeks and try different options. Maybe you want to keep going, using just the habits that made the biggest difference. The choice is yours!

A list of ten commitments can feel like a solid starting place, but you might have five core principles, or twenty-five promises might be more your speed. You can create a permanent list, or you can do what I like to do, which is to create a list for a specific year. For example, in 2019 I made myself a *19 for 2019* list. I redo it annually because I continue learning about myself and learning new tips and tricks.

Here's my 20 for 2020 list.

1. Read every day.
2. Drink at least sixty-four ounces of water per day.
3. Choose sleep. Always.
4. Walk 10,000 steps a day at least five days a week.
5. Do yoga, lift weights, or bike at least three days a week.
6. Have an uninterrupted date night with my husband every week.
7. Engage in much less internet phone scrolling.
8. Explore Denver like a tourist.
9. Take a trip, for pleasure, by myself.
10. Meditate every morning.
11. Choose healthy fats and protein; limit sugar intake.
12. Take a gratitude photo every day.
13. Eat at home more often than out.
14. Learn how to make a new meal.
15. Read more poetry.
16. Begin researching my next book.
17. Write more thank-you cards.
18. Embrace boredom.
19. Eat without distractions.
20. Keep promises to myself.

You might also consider choosing a theme word or phrase for your new school year. My word for this year is *unstoppable*. In the past, I've chosen *transform*, *gratitude*, and *growth*. I know other people who have chosen *simplicity*, *focus*, *loosen up*, *play*, *balance*, and *calm*.

Final Reflection

After working through these thirty-six weeks, set aside time to make final reflections on this 180-day journey as a whole. Remember when I asked you—*before* you started your journey—to reflect on how satisfied you were with your self-care? Take a look at your notes in the introduction (pages 7–8) and consider how you feel now. Is there a positive difference? You may choose to do some free writing, or you might want to answer some of the questions I've included here.

Reflect on your initial satisfaction with your self-care (on a scale of 1 to 10). Where would you place yourself now? What is the biggest difference in your overall health and well-being?

....

....

What were the changes that you wanted to make? Were you able to make them?

....

....

What currently brings you joy in your life? Is this the same or different than what brought you joy the first time I asked you this question?

....

....

Who supported you on your journey? How did they support you? How can you show your appreciation?

....

....

What was your greatest hope when doing this work? Did you reach your goal?

....

....

As you reflect on the last 180 days, what are you proudest of?

....

....

What were your biggest challenges while doing this work, and what did you learn from them?

....

....

What are you most excited about? What new habits and practices mean the most to you or have had the greatest impact on you?

....

....

As you think about the next 180 days, what will self-care look like? How can you keep your promises to yourself?

....

....

What else do you want to remember about this journey? Record any additional closing thoughts here.

....

....

References and Resources

40 for 40. (n.d.). In *Facebook*. Accessed at https://facebook.com/unplug40for40 on March 15, 2019.

Achor, S. (2011a). *The happiness advantage: The seven principles that fuel success and performance at work*. London: Virgin.

Achor, S. (2011b). *The happy secret to better work* [Video file]. Accessed at www.ted.com/talks/shawn_achor_the_happy_secret_to_better_work?language=en on June 21, 2019.

Ackerman, C. (2017a). *28 benefits of gratitude and most significant research findings*. Accessed at https://positivepsychologyprogram.com/benefits-gratitude-research-questions on March 15, 2019.

Ackerman, C. (2017b). *23 amazing health benefits of mindfulness for body and brain*. Accessed at https://positivepsychologyprogram.com/benefits-of-mindfulness on May 19, 2019.

Addiction Resource. (2017). *Social media addiction—The facts and solutions*. Accessed at https://addictionresource.com/addiction/technology-addiction/social-media-addiction on June 21, 2019.

Adichie, C. N. (2004). *Purple hibiscus*. London: Fourth Estate.

Adventure. (n.d.). In *Merriam-Webster online*. Accessed at https://merriam-webster.com/dictionary/adventure on March 15, 2019.

Aldrup, K., Klusmann, U., Lüdtke, O., Göllner, R., & Trautwein, U. (2018). Student misbehavior and teacher well-being: Testing the mediating role of the teacher-student relationship. *Learning and Instruction*, *58*, 126–136. Accessed at www.sciencedirect.com/science/article/pii/S0959475217302645 on April 15, 2019.

American Psychological Association. (2006). *Multitasking: Switching costs*. Accessed at www.apa.org/research/action/multitask on April 21, 2019.

Anxiety Canada. (n.d.). *Calm breathing.* Accessed at www.anxietycanada.com/sites /default/files/CalmBreathing.pdf on March 18, 2019.

Anzia, N. (2018). Life is easier with a capsule wardrobe. *Washington Post.* Accessed at https://washingtonpost.com/lifestyle/home/life-is-easier-with-a-capsule -wardrobe/2018/05/07/708d5b14-4d74-11e8-b725-92c89fe3ca4c_story.html ?utm_term=.6bb251c84489 on March 15, 2019.

Asano, E. (2017). *How much time do people spend on social media?* Accessed at www .socialmediatoday.com/marketing/how-much-time-do-people-spend-social-media -infographic on June 21, 2019.

Beah, I. (2007). *A long way gone: Memoirs of a boy soldier.* New York: Sarah Crichton Books.

Bergland, C. (2014). Maintaining healthy social connections improves well-being [Blog post]. *Psychology Today.* Accessed at https://psychologytoday.com/us/blog /the-athletes-way/201402/maintaining-healthy-social-connections-improves -well-being on March 15, 2019.

Bhavsar, A. (2017). *Be successful: Thrive exponentially beyond excellence.* Ahmedabad, Gujarat, India: Be An Author.

Blakeman, B. (2018). *I sip my iced coffee from these stylish (ecofriendly) straws.* Accessed at http://nymag.com/strategist/article/best-metal-straws-review.html on April 18, 2019.

Blikman, C. (n.d.). *How to stop saying yes when you want to say no.* Accessed at tinybuddha.com/blog/stop-saying-yes-want-say-no on June 19, 2019.

Boogren, T. H. (2018). *Take time for you: Self-care action plans for educators.* Bloomington, IN: Solution Tree Press.

Briggs, S. (2015). *Refuse to be a boring teacher: 15 ways to have more fun.* Accessed at www.opencolleges.edu.au/informed/features/refuse-to-be-a-boring-teacher on June 21, 2019.

Brosh, A. (2016). *5 questions to ask yourself before posting to social media* [Blog post]. Accessed at https://healthyway.com/content/5-questions-to-ask-yourself-before -posting-to-social-media on March 15, 2019.

Brown, B. (2010). *The gifts of imperfection: Let go of who you think you're supposed to be and embrace who you are.* Center City, MN: Hazelden.

Brown, B. (2018). *Dare to lead: Brave work. Tough conversations. Whole hearts.* New York: Random House.

Brown, S. (2008). *Play is more than just fun* [Video file]. Accessed at https://ted.com /talks/stuart_brown_says_play_is_more_than_fun_it_s_vital on March 15, 2019.

Buckley, A. (n.d.). Yoga for kids [Slideshow]. *Parents*. Accessed at https://parents .com/fun/activities/indoor/yoga-for-kids on March 15, 2019.

Burchard, B. (2017). *High performance habits: How extraordinary people become that way*. Carlsbad, CA: Hay House.

Büssing, A., Michalsen, A., Khalsa, S. B. S., Telles, S., & Sherman, K. J. (2012). Effects of yoga on mental and physical health: A short summary of reviews. *Evidence-Based Complementary and Alternative Medicine*. Accessed at www.hindawi.com/journals/ecam/2012/165410 on April 19, 2019.

Cacioppo, J. T., & Patrick, W. (2008). *Loneliness: Human nature and the need for social connection*. New York: Norton.

Casey, S. (2017). *2016 Nielsen social media report*. Accessed at www.nielsen.com/us /en/insights/reports/2017/2016-nielsen-social-media-report.html on April 21, 2019.

Chattu, V. K., Manzar, D., Kumary, S., Burman, D., Spence, D. W., & Pandi-Perumal, S. R. (2018). The global problem of insufficient sleep and its serious public health implications. *Healthcare, 7*(1). Accessed at www.mdpi.com/2227 -9032/7/1/1/htm on April 15, 2019.

Collingwood, J. (2018). *Learning to say no*. Accessed at https://psychcentral.com/lib /learning-to-say-no on March 15, 2019.

Cook, K. (2017). *Mindful moments*. Accessed at www.ckgfoundation.org /speakupnewsblog/a-mindful-moment on April 19, 2019.

Cristallo, M. (n.d.). *25 simple things you can do to get inspired*. Accessed at https:// lifehack.org/articles/communication/25-simple-things-you-can-get-inspired.html on March 15, 2019.

Csikszentmihalyi, M. (2008). *Flow: The psychology of optimal experience*. New York: Harper Perennial.

Daly, A. J., & Finnigan, K. S. (2010). The ebb and flow of social network ties between district leaders under high-stakes accountability. *American Educational Research Journal, 48*(1), 39–79.

Day, C., & Leitch, R. (2001). Teachers' and teacher educators' lives: The role of emotion. *Teaching and Teacher Education, 17*(4), 403–415.

Doland, E. (2019). *Saying "no."* Accessed at https://unclutterer.com/2019/02/22 /saying-no on August 19, 2019.

Doraiswamy, P. M., & Agronin, M. E. (2009). Brain games: Do they really work? *Scientific American*. Accessed at https://scientificamerican.com/article/brain-games-do-they-really on March 15, 2019.

Doskoch, P. (2016). Happily ever laughter. *Psychology Today*. Accessed at www.psychologytoday.com/us/articles/199607/happily-ever-laughter on June 21, 2019.

Dove, L. L. (n.d.). *Why do rhymes help people remember things?* Accessed at science.howstuffworks.com/life/inside-the-mind/human-brain/why-do-rhymes-help-people-remember-things.htm on June 21, 2019.

Drake, C., Roehrs, T., Shambroom, J., & Roth, T. (2013). Caffeine effects on sleep taken 0, 3, or 6 hours before going to bed. *Journal of Clinical Sleep Medicine, 9*(11), 1195–2000. Accessed at https://ncbi.nlm.nih.gov/pubmed/24235903 on November 8, 2017.

Duhigg, C. (2012). *The power of habit: Why we do what we do in life and business.* New York: Random House.

Emmons, R. A., & McCullough, M. E. (2003). Counting blessings versus burdens: An experimental investigation of gratitude and subjective well-being in daily life. *Journal of Personality and Social Psychology, 84*(2), 377–389. Accessed at https://ncbi.nlm.nih.gov/pubmed/12585811 on March 15, 2019.

Eric, D. (2019). *George Saunders finds inspiration at the mall.* Accessed at https://electricliterature.com/george-saunders-finds-inspiration-at-the-mall/ on April 21, 2019.

Ericson, C. (2014). 5 ways to take control of your email inbox. *Forbes*. Accessed at www.forbes.com/sites/learnvest/2014/03/17/5-ways-to-take-control-of-your-email-inbox/#6063442d6342 on June 21, 2019.

Fábrega, M. (n.d.). *How to laugh more—22 ways to bring more laughter into your life* [Blog post]. Accessed at https://daringtolivefully.com/how-to-laugh-more on March 15, 2019.

Farnam Street. (2017). *The keys to happiness* [Blog post]. Accessed at https://fs.blog/2014/10/the-keys-to-happiness on March 18, 2019.

Felver, J. C., Butzer, B., Olson, K. J., Smith, I. M., & Khalsa, S. B. S. (2015). Yoga in public school improves adolescent mood and affect. *Contemporary School Psychology, 19*(3), 184–192.

Finnegan, W. (2015). *Barbarian days: A surfing life.* New York: Penguin Press.

Gallup. (2014). *State of America's schools: The path to winning again in education.* Accessed at www.gallup.com/services/178769/state-america-schools-report.aspx on March 15, 2019.

Gilbert, E. (2009). *Your elusive creative genius* [Video file]. Accessed at www.ted.com /talks/elizabeth_gilbert_on_genius?language=en on June 21, 2019.

Gilman, A. (2018). 13 ways to bring hygge to your classroom. *We Are Teachers.* Accessed at www.weareteachers.com/classroom-hygge on April 21, 2019.

Goetz, T. (2016). How to change unhealthy habits [Blog post]. *Psychology Today.* Accessed at https://psychologytoday.com/us/blog/renaissance-woman/201607 /how-change-unhealthy-habits on March 15, 2019.

Gonzalez, J. (2015). *5 powerful ways to save time as a teacher* [Blog post]. Accessed at https://cultofpedagogy.com/40hour on March 15, 2019.

Granata, K. (2014). Teacher stress and disengagement impacts student performance. *Education World.* Accessed at www.educationworld.com/a_curr/teacher-stress -impacts-student-performance.shtml on March 15, 2019.

Gunn, J. (2018). Self-care for teachers of traumatized students [Blog post]. *Concordia Room 241.* Accessed at https://education.cu-portland.edu/blog/classroom -resources/self-care-for-teachers on April 15, 2019.

Hamady, J. (2015). The importance of rest [Blog post]. *Psychology Today.* Accessed at https://psychologytoday.com/us/blog/finding-your-voice/201507/the- importance-rest on March 15, 2019.

Hampton, D. (2016). *How listening to music benefits your brain.* Accessed at https:// thebestbrainpossible.com/how-listening-to-music-benefits-your-brain on March 15, 2019.

Happier in Hollywood. (2018). *Episode 71: Take an obligation vacation* [Podcast]. Accessed at http://happierinhollywood.com/episode71 on March 15, 2019.

Hardy, B. (2017). *Why keeping a daily journal could change your life* [Blog post]. Accessed at https://medium.com/the-mission/why-keeping-a-daily-journal -could-change-your-life-9a4c11f1a475 on March 15, 2019.

Harvard Health Publishing. (2016). *8 steps to mindful eating.* Accessed at www.health .harvard.edu/staying-healthy/8-steps-to-mindful-eating on March 18, 2019.

Harvard Health Publishing. (2018a). *Blue light has a dark side.* Accessed at www .health.harvard.edu/staying-healthy/blue-light-has-a-dark-side on May 1, 2019.

Harvard Health Publishing. (2018b). *Relaxation techniques: Breath control helps quell errant stress response.* Accessed at https://health.harvard.edu/mind-and-mood /relaxation-techniques-breath-control-helps-quell-errant-stress-response on April 18, 2019.

Healthline Editorial Team. (n.d.). *Mood food: Can what you eat affect your happiness?* Accessed at https://healthline.com/health/mood-food-can-what-you-eat-affect -your-happiness on March 15, 2019.

HelpGuide. (n.d.). *Benefits of mindfulness: Practices for improving emotional and physical well-being.* Accessed at https://helpguide.org/harvard/benefits-of -mindfulness.htm?pdf=14945 on March 15, 2019.

Herrera, T. (2018). How to ask for help and actually get it. *The New York Times.* Accessed at www.nytimes.com/2018/08/20/smarter-living/how-to-ask-for-help -and-actually-get-it.html on June 21, 2019.

Heston, K. (2019). How to be creative. *WikiHow.* Accessed at https://wikihow.com /Be-Creative on March 15, 2019.

Hillman, G., & Stalets, M. (2019). *Coaching your classroom: How to deliver actionable feedback to students.* Bloomington, IN: Solution Tree Press.

Hirschlag, A. (2017). 6 relaxation hacks for people who hate meditating. *HuffPost.* Accessed at www.huffpost.com/entry/meditation-alternatives_n_592371a9e4b0 94cdba56d8a2 on May 1, 2019.

Hollis, R. (n.d.). *#Last90Days Challenge.* Accessed at https://thechicsite.com/90days on March 15, 2019.

HuffPost. (2014). *20 simple ways to treat yourself for under $20.* Accessed at https:// huffingtonpost.com/2014/06/23/rewards-under-20_n_5045417.html on March 15, 2019.

Hutton, L. (n.d.). 18 simple ways to put laughter back into your life. *Lifehack.* Accessed at https://lifehack.org/articles/communication/18-simple-ways-put -laughter-back-into-your-life.html on March 15, 2019.

Iberlin, J. M. (2017). *Cultivating mindfulness in the classroom.* Bloomington, IN: Marzano Resources.

Immordino-Yang, M. H., Christodoulou, J. A., & Singh, V. (2012). Rest is not idleness: Implications of the brain's default mode for human development and education. *Perspectives on Psychological Science, 7*(4), 352–364.

Jabr, F. (2013). Why your brain needs more downtime. *Scientific American.* Accessed at www.scientificamerican.com/article/mental-downtime on April 21, 2019.

Jacobs, A. J. (2014). How to be more creative. *Real Simple*. Accessed at https://realsimple.com/health/mind-mood/how-to-be-creative on March 15, 2019.

Jan, M., Soomro, S. A., & Ahmad, N. (2017). Impact of social media on self-esteem. *European Scientific Journal*, *13*(23), 329–341.

Johnson, R. A., Odendaal, J. S. J., & Meadows, R. L. (2002). Animal-assisted interventions research: Issues and answers. *Western Journal of Nursing Research*, *24*(4), 422–440.

Joiner, B. (2018). *The 5 productive morning routines of highly effective people* [Video blog post]. Accessed at https://blog.trello.com/best-productive-morning-routines on March 15, 2019.

Kabat-Zinn, J. (2003). Mindfulness-based interventions in context: Past, present, and future. *Clinical Psychology: Science and Practice*, *10*(2), 144–156.

Kalanithi, P. (2016). *When breath becomes air*. New York: Random House.

Kane, S. (2018). *Best ways to spend idle time*. Accessed at https://psychcentral.com/lib/best-ways-to-spend-idle-time on March 15, 2019.

Kashyap, V. (2018). *Psychology hacks to increase your creativity and productivity*. Accessed at https://medium.com/thrive-global/psychology-hacks-to-increase-your-creativity-and-productivity-e4427feea4c on June 21, 2019.

Kaufman, S. B. (2011). Why inspiration matters. *Harvard Business Review*. Accessed at https://hbr.org/2011/11/why-inspiration-matters on March 15, 2019.

Khosla, P. (2017). Everything is terrible but today is 'treat yo self' day, so go wild. *Mashable*. Accessed at https://mashable.com/2017/10/13/treat-yo-self-day-parks-rec/#W.O32kVjWiqF on March 15, 2019.

Kondō, M. (2014). *The life-changing magic of tidying up: The Japanese art of decluttering and organizing*. Berkeley, CA: Ten Speed Press.

Kreider, T. (2012, June 30). The "busy" trap [Blog post]. *The New York Times*. Accessed at https://opinionator.blogs.nytimes.com/2012/06/30/the-busy-trap on March 15, 2019.

Kunnari, I., & Lipponen, L. (2010). Building teacher-student relationships for wellbeing. *Lifelong Learning in Europe*, *XV*, 63–71.

Kurtz, J. L. (2015). Six reasons to get a hobby [Blog post]. *Psychology Today*. Accessed at https://psychologytoday.com/us/blog/happy-trails/201509/six-reasons-get-hobby on March 15, 2019.

Ladika, S. (2018). *Technology addiction*. Accessed at library.cqpress.com/cqresearcher/document.php?id=cqresrre2018042000 on June 21, 2019.

Lamott, A. (2017). *12 truths I learned from life and writing* [Video file]. Accessed at www.ted.com/talks/anne_lamott_12_truths_i_learned_from_life_and_writing on June 21, 2019.

Lee, I. F. (2018). *Where joy hides and how to find it* [Video file]. Accessed at www.ted .com/talks/ingrid_fetell_lee_where_joy_hides_and_how_to_find_it?language=en on June 21, 2019.

Leech, J. (2017). 7 science-based health benefits of drinking enough water. *Healthline*. Accessed at https://healthline.com/nutrition/7-health-benefits-of -water on March 15, 2019.

Levin, M. (2018). 5 steps to an effective accountability partnership, and 2 things to never do. *Inc.* Accessed at www.inc.com/marissa-levin/5-ways-to-make-your -accountability-partnership-work-2-ways-to-ruin-it.html on June 19, 2019.

Lieberman, M. D. (2013). *Social: Why our brains are wired to connect.* New York: Broadway Books.

Lin, H. L. (2012). How your cell phone hurts your relationships. *Scientific American.* Accessed at www.scientificamerican.com/article/how-your-cell-phone-hurts -your-relationships on March 15, 2019.

Luyster, F. S., Strollo, P. J., Zee, P. C., & Walsh, J. K. (2012). Sleep: A health imperative. *Sleep, 35*(6), 727–734.

Marcin, A. (n.d.). *10 things that happen to your body when you lose sleep.* Accessed at https://healthline.com/health/healthy-sleep/what-happens-to-your-body-when -you-lose-sleep#1 on March 15, 2019.

Mark, J. (2017). Get out of here: Scientists examine the benefits of forests, birdsong and running water. *The New York Times.* Accessed at https://nytimes .com/2017/03/02/books/review/nature-fix-florence-williams.html on March 15, 2019.

Martin, A. (2006). The relationship between teachers' perceptions of student motivation and engagement and teachers' enjoyment of and confidence in teaching. *Asia-Pacific Journal of Teacher Education, 34*(1), 73–93.

Mason, C., Rivers Murphy, M. M., & Jackson, Y. (2019). *Mindfulness practices: Cultivating heart centered communities where students focus and flourish.* Bloomington, IN: Solution Tree Press.

Matthews, L. (2018). What is hygge? Everything you need to know about the Danish lifestyle trend. *Country Living.* Accessed at https://countryliving.com /life/a41187/what-is-hygge-things-to-know-about-the-danish-lifestyle-trend on March 15, 2019.

Mayo Clinic Staff. (2016). *Stress relief from laughter? It's no joke.* Accessed at https://mayoclinic.org/healthy-lifestyle/stress-management/in-depth/stress-relief/art-20044456 on March 18, 2019.

Miller, J. M. (2018). *How to be present in the moment (and why it's SO important).* [Blog post]. Accessed at https://psychcentral.com/blog/how-to-be-present-in-the-moment-and-why-its-so-important on March 15, 2019.

Mogilner, C. (2010). The pursuit of happiness: Time, money, and social connection. *Psychological Science, 21*(9), 1348–1354.

Moir, E. (2011, August). *Phases of first-year teaching* [Blog post]. Accessed at https://newteachercenter.org/blog/2011/08/17/phases-of-first-year-teaching on October 18, 2017.

Morin, A. (2015). 7 scientifically proven benefits of gratitude [Blog post]. *Psychology Today.* Accessed at https://psychologytoday.com/us/blog/what-mentally-strong-people-dont-do/201504/7-scientifically-proven-benefits-gratitude on March 18, 2019.

Naidoo, U. (2018). *Gut feelings: How food affects your mood.* Accessed at www.health.harvard.edu/blog/gut-feelings-how-food-affects-your-mood-2018120715548 on June 19, 2019.

National Institute on Aging. (n.d.). *A good night's sleep.* Accessed at www.nia.nih.gov/health/good-nights-sleep on April 21, 2019.

New Teacher Center. (2016). *New teacher development for every inning.* Accessed at https://newteachercenter.org/wp-content/uploads/NewTeacherDevelopmentEveryInning.pdf on June 21, 2019.

Nguyen, T. (2015). *10 surprising benefits you'll get from keeping a journal* [Blog post]. Accessed at https://huffpost.com/entry/benefits-of-journaling_b_6648884 on March 28, 2019.

Northwestern Medicine. (n.d.). *5 benefits of healthy relationships.* Accessed at http://nmbreakthroughs.org/wellness/5-benefits-of-healthy-relationships on March 18, 2019.

O'Connor, K. E. (2008). "You choose to care": Teachers, emotions and professional identity. *Teaching and Teacher Education, 24*(1), 117–126.

O'Connor, E. E., Dearing, E., & Collins, B. A. (2011). Teacher-child relationship and behavior problem trajectories in elementary school. *American Educational Research Journal, 48*(1), 120–162.

Offline October. (n.d.). *Don't post a story live one.* Accessed at https://offlineoctober.com on March 18, 2019.

Park, D. C., Lodi-Smith, J., Drew, L., Haber, S., Hebrank, A. Bischof, G. N., et al. (2014). The impact of sustained engagement on cognitive function in older adults: The synapse project. *Psychological Science, 25*(1), 103–112.

Pasricha, N. (n.d.). *7 ways to be happy right now.* Accessed at https://globalhappiness .org/7-ways-to-be-happy-right-now on March 18, 2019.

Pasricha, N. (2016). *The happiness equation: Want nothing + do anything = have everything.* New York: G. P. Putnam's Sons.

Pay It Forward Day. (n.d.). *The ripple effect continues! Sunday, April 28, 2019.* Accessed at http://payitforwardday.com on March 18, 2019.

Pierce, S. (2013). Make over your mornings for a more productive year. *HuffPost.* Accessed at https://huffingtonpost.com/stacia-pierce/make-over-your-mornings -f_b_4495018.html on March 18, 2019.

Price, C. (2018). *How to break up with your phone: The 30-day plan to take back your life.* London: Trapeze.

Purcell, M. (2018). The health benefits of journaling. *Psych Central.* Accessed at https://psychcentral.com/lib/the-health-benefits-of-journaling on March 18, 2019.

Quotefancy. (n.d.). *7 wallpapers.* Accessed at https://quotefancy.com/quote/777669 /Bren-Brown-Laughter-song-and-dance-create-emotional-and-spiritual -connection-they-remind on March 18, 2019.

Raes, F., Griffith, J. W., Van der Gucht, K., & Williams, J. M. G. (2014). School-based prevention and reduction of depression in adolescents: A cluster-randomized controlled trial of a mindfulness group program. *Mindfulness, 5*(5), 477–486.

Raphael, J. R. (2017). *The 7-step guide to achieving inbox zero—and staying there— in 2018.* Accessed at https://fastcompany.com/40507663/the-7-step-guide-to -achieving-inbox-zero-and-staying-there-in-2018 on March 18, 2019.

Real Simple. (2008). *Too much stuff?* Accessed at www.greensboro.com/life/too -much-stuff/article_f1fd35f7-2184-5434-b1a6-571bca1ff8c7.amp.html on April 21, 2019.

Remen, R. N. (2006). *Kitchen table wisdom: Stories that heal.* New York: Riverhead Books.

Restak, R. (2009). *Think smart: A neuroscientist's prescription for improving your brain's performance.* New York: Riverhead Books.

Riley, P. (2018). *The Australian principal occupational health, safety and wellbeing survey: 2017 data.* Accessed at www.principalhealth.org/au/2017_Report_AU _FINAL.pdf on June 19, 2019.

Riley-Missouri, C. (2018). Lots of teachers are super stressed out. *Futurity.* Accessed at https://futurity.org/teachers-stress-1739832 on March 18, 2019.

Rizzo, K. (2017). Why asking for help is a strength (and three ways to do so effectively). *Forbes.* Accessed at https://forbes.com/sites/forbescoachescouncil /2017/09/15/why-asking-for-help-is-a-strength-and-three-ways-to-do-so-effectively /#252fdfd572b7 on March 18, 2019.

Robbins, M. (2011). *It's OK to ask for help* [Blog post]. Accessed at https://huffpost .com/entry/asking-for-help-ok_b_814796 on March 18, 2019.

Robert Wood Johnson Foundation. (2017). *Traumatic experiences widespread among U.S. youth, new data show.* Accessed at www.rwjf.org/en/library/articles-and -news/2017/10/traumatic-experiences-widespread-among-u-s--youth--new-data -show.html on April 15, 2019.

Robinson, N. (2018). Looming crisis in school leadership: One in five principals is burnt out [Blog post]. *ABC Education.* Accessed at http://education.abc.net.au /newsandarticles/blog/-/b/2802427/looming-crisis-in-school-leadership-one-in -five-principals-is-burnt-out on March 18, 2019.

Rouse, M. (2014). *Inbox zero.* Accessed at https://whatis.techtarget.com/definition /inbox-zero on March 18, 2019.

Royer, H., Stehr, M., & Sydnor, J. (2015). Incentives, commitments, and habit formation in exercise: Evidence from a field experiment with workers at a Fortune-500 company. *American Economic Journal: Applied Economics, 7*(3), 51–84.

Rubin, G. (2006). *Need a simple and effective way to get your life under control? Try the "one-minute rule."* [Blog post]. Accessed at https://gretchenrubin.com/2006/12 /need_a_simple_a on March 18, 2019.

Rubin, G. (2014). *Secret of adulthood: Outer order contributes to inner calm* [Blog post]. Accessed at https://gretchenrubin.com/2014/05/secret-of-adulthood -outer-order-contributes-to-inner-calm on March 18, 2019.

Rubin, G. (2015). *Better than before: Mastering the habits of our everyday lives* [Audible version]. New York: Random House Audio.

Ryan, J. (n.d.). *Balancing blood sugar.* Accessed at www.drjeanetteryan.com /condition/balancing-blood-sugar on June 2, 2019.

Ryan, R. M., & Deci, E. L. (2000a). Intrinsic and extrinsic motivations: Classic definitions and new directions. *Contemporary Educational Psychology, 25*(1), 54–67.

Ryan, R. M., & Deci, E. L. (2000b). Self-determination theory and the facilitation of intrinsic motivation, social development, and well-being. *American Psychologist, 55*(1), 68–78.

Salcius, D. (n.d.). *The art of paying it forward without spending a dime* [Blog post]. Accessed at https://medium.com/the-designing-north-project/the-art-of-paying -it-forward-without-spending-a-dime-e75a7b040fdb on May 19, 2019.

Schwartz, B. (2016). *The paradox of choice: Why more is less* (Rev. ed.). New York: HarperCollins.

Scott, E. (2018). *5 self-care practices for every area of your life.* Accessed at https:// verywellmind.com/self-care-strategies-overall-stress-reduction-3144729 on March 18, 2019.

Scott, S. J. (2019). *51 daily morning routine habits for an amazing start to your day.* Accessed at https://developgoodhabits.com/morning-routine-habits on March 18, 2019.

Semple, R. J., Droutman, V., & Reid, B. A. (2017). Mindfulness goes to school: Things learned (so far) from research and real-world experiences. *Psychology in the Schools, 54*(1), 29–52.

Sepel, J. (n.d.). *Rest: The importance of slowing down.* Accessed at https:// mindbodygreen.com/0-6182/Rest-The-Importance-of-Slowing-Down.html on March 18, 2019.

Smith, J. (2012). Steve Jobs always dressed exactly the same. Here's who else does. *Forbes.* Accessed at https://forbes.com/sites/jacquelynsmith/2012/10/05/steve -jobs-always-dressed-exactly-the-same-heres-who-else-does on March 18, 2019.

Smith, M., Robinson, L., & Segal, R. (2018). How to sleep better: Simple steps to getting a good night's sleep. *HelpGuide.* Accessed at https://helpguide.org /articles/sleep/getting-better-sleep.htm on March 18, 2019.

Smith, M., Robinson, L., & Segal, J. (2019). Preventing Alzheimer's disease. *HelpGuide.* Accessed at https://helpguide.org/articles/alzheimers-dementia-aging /preventing-alzheimers-disease.htm on March 18, 2019.

Sofer, O. J. (2016). *The practice of walking.* Accessed at www.mindfulschools.org /personal-practice/walking on March 18, 2019.

Spilt, J. L., Koomen, H. M. Y., & Thijs, J. T. (2011). Teacher wellbeing: The importance of teacher-student relationships. *Educational Psychology Review, 23*(4), 457–477.

Strober, E. (2016, June 28). *5 problems with social media* [Blog post]. Accessed at https://theodysseyonline.com/five-problems-with-social-media on March 18, 2019.

TakeLessons. (n.d.). *11 surprising health benefits of singing.* Accessed at takelessons .com/live/singing/health-benefits-of-singing on June 21, 2019.

Tartakovsky, M. (2018, July 8). The importance of play for adults. *Psych Central.* Accessed at https://psychcentral.com/blog/the-importance-of-play-for-adults on March 18, 2019.

Tennstedt, S. L., & Unverzagt, F. W. (2013). The ACTIVE study: Study overview and major findings. *Journal of Aging and Health, 25*(8), 3S–20S.

Text Request. (2017). *How much time do people spend on their mobile phones in 2017?* Accessed at https://hackernoon.com/how-much-time-do-people-spend-on-their -mobile-phones-in-2017-e5f90a0b10a6 on March 15, 2019.

Tierney, J. (2011). Do you suffer from decision fatigue? *The New York Times.* Accessed at www.nytimes.com/2011/08/21/magazine/do-you-suffer-from-decision -fatigue.html on June 21, 2019.

Timmons, J. (2019). *The best hydration apps of 2019.* Accessed at https://healthline .com/health/hydration-top-iphone-android-apps-drinking-water#ihydrate on August 7, 2019.

University of Rochester Medical Center. (n.d.). *Journaling for mental health.* Accessed at https://urmc.rochester.edu/encyclopedia/content.aspx ?ContentID=4552&ContentTypeID=1 on March 15, 2019.

Vesely, A. K., Saklofske, D. H., & Leschied, A. D. W. (2013). Teachers—The vital resource: The contribution of emotional intelligence to teacher efficacy and well-being. *Canadian Journal of School Psychology, 28*(1), 71–89.

Vigil, B. (2018, May 16). *100+ awesome summer bucket list ideas* [Blog post]. Accessed at https://playpartyplan.com/summer-bucket-list-ideas on March 18, 2019.

Vozza, S. (2016). *The ultimate guide to saying no to things you don't want to do.* Accessed at www.fastcompany.com/3056562/the-ultimate-guide-to-saying-no-to-things -you-dont-want-to on June 19, 2019.

Wall, A. (2018). How busy hands can alter our brain chemistry. *CBS News.* Accessed at www.cbsnews.com/news/handiwork-how-busy-hands-can-alter-our-brain -chemistry on May 19, 2019.

Walls, J. (2006). *The glass castle: a memoir.* New York: Scribner.

Walton, A. G. (2017). 6 ways social media affects our mental health. *Forbes.* Accessed at https://forbes.com/sites/alicegwalton/2017/06/30/a-run-down-of-social -medias-effects-on-our-mental-health/#1a17a2072e5a on March 18, 2019.

Westover, T. (2018). *Educated: A memoir*. New York: Random House.

Whillans, A. V., Weidman, A. C., & Dunn, E. W. (2016). Valuing time over money is associated with greater happiness. *Social Psychological and Personality Science*, *7*(3), 213–222.

Wiking, M. (2017). *The little book of hygge: Danish secrets to happy living*. New York: HarperCollins.

Williams, F. (2017). *The nature fix: Why nature makes us happier, healthier, and more creative*. New York: Norton.

Winston D. (n.d.). *Guided meditations* [Podcast]. Accessed at http://marc.ucla.edu/mindful-meditations on March 15, 2019.

Wolff, C. (2016). 10 ways to have a healthy relationship with social media. *Bustle*. Accessed at https://bustle.com/articles/164876-10-ways-to-have-a-healthy-relationship-with-social-media on March 18, 2019.

World Counts. (n.d.). *Habits are very important*. Accessed at http://theworldcounts.com/life/potentials/the-importance-of-good-habits on March 15, 2019.

World Health Organization. (2016). *Child maltreatment*. Accessed at www.who.int/en/news-room/fact-sheets/detail/child-maltreatment on April 15, 2019.

World Sleep Day. (n.d.). *Talking points*. Accessed at http://worldsleepday.org/usetoolkit/talking-points on April 16, 2019.

Yang, A. (Writer), & McDougall, C. (Director). (2011). Pawnee rangers [Television series episode]. In Daniels, G., Schur, M., Klein, H., Miner, D., Sackett, M., Holland, D., & Goor, D. (Executive Producers), *Parks and recreation*. New York: National Broadcasting Company (NBC). Accessed at www.imdb.com/title/tt2041051 on March 15, 2019.

Yoshimoto, B. (2016). *Moshi moshi*. Berkeley, CA: Counterpoint.

Yousafzai, M. (2013). *I am Malala: The girl who stood up for education and was shot by the Taliban*. New York: Little, Brown.

Zomorodi, M. (2017). *How boredom can lead to your most brilliant ideas* [Video file]. Accessed at www.ted.com/talks/manoush_zomorodi_how_boredom_can_lead_to_your_most_brilliant_ideas?language=en on May 3, 2019.

Index

Take Time for You
Tina H. Boogren

The key to thriving as a human and an educator rests in self-care. With *Take Time for You*, you'll discover a clear path to well-being. The author offers manageable strategies, reflection questions, and surveys that will guide you in developing an individualized self-care plan.

BKF813

The Beginning Teacher's Field Guide
Tina H. Boogren

The joys and pains of starting a teaching career often go undiscussed. This guide explores the personal side of teaching, offering crucial advice and support. The author details six phases every new teacher goes through and outlines classroom strategies and self-care practices.

BKF806

Supporting Beginning Teachers
Tina H. Boogren

Give new teachers the time and professional guidance they need to become expert teachers through effective mentoring. Investigate key research and examine the four types of support—physical, emotional, instructional, and institutional—that are crucial during a teacher's first year in the classroom.

BKL023

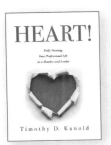

HEART!
Timothy D. Kanold

Explore the concept of a heartprint—the distinctive impression an educator's heart leaves on students and colleagues during his or her professional career. Use this resource to reflect on your professional journey and discover how to foster productive, heart-centered classrooms and schools.

BKF749

Solution Tree | Press
a division of
Solution Tree

Visit SolutionTree.com or call 800.733.6786 to order.

Wait! Your professional development journey doesn't have to end with the last pages of this book.

We realize improving student learning doesn't happen overnight. And your school or district shouldn't be left to puzzle out all the details of this process alone.

No matter where you are on the journey, we're committed to helping you get to the next stage.

Take advantage of everything from **custom workshops** to **keynote presentations** and **interactive web and video conferencing**. We can even help you develop an action plan tailored to fit your specific needs.

Let's get the conversation started.

Call 888.763.9045 today.